Stardust

Stardust

BRUCE SERAFIN

Vancouver
New Star Books
2007

NEW STAR BOOKS LTD.
107 – 3477 Commercial Street | Vancouver, BC V5N 4E8   CANADA
1574 Gulf Road, #1517 | Point Roberts, WA 98281   USA
www.NewStarBooks.com | info@NewStarBooks.com

We acknowledge the financial support of the Canada Council, the Government of Canada through the Book Publishing Industry Development Program, the British Columbia Arts Council, and the Government of British Columbia through the Book Publishing Tax Credit.

Cover by Mutasis.com
Printed and bound in Canada by Imprimerie Gauvin, Gatineau, QC
First printing, October 2007

LIBRARY AND ARCHIVES CANADA
CATALOGUING IN PUBLICATION

Serafin, Bruce
    Stardust / Bruce Serafin.

ISBN 978-1-55420-033-7

    I. Title.
PS8587.E695A16 2007   C814'.6   C2007–904649–5

Recycled
Supporting responsible use
of forest resources
www.fsc.org Cert no. SGS-COC-2624
© 1996 Forest Stewardship Council
FSC
100%

For my dear Sharon

For Stan

Contents

Acknowledgments

Early versions of "Stan Persky's Enormous Reasonableness" and "Avant-Garde Mentalities" appeared in *Books in Canada*. "Sailors" first appeared on www.thetyee.ca. "The Crosses" and "Dead on the Shelf" first appeared in the original *Vancouver Review*. "The Secret", "Vermeer's Patch", "Cowboy Stories", "Long Tall Sally", "A Chest of Drawers", "Glavin's Progress", "Wearing a Mask", "Stardust", "Leetle Bateese", and "The Crosses" were first published on www.dooneyscafe.com.

The author would like to thank Stan Persky, Rolf Maurer and Carellin Brooks for their zeal, professionalism and kindness.

Stardust

The Alley

1

On sunny afternoons when my work as a mailhandler was done, I wrote in the lunchroom at Vancouver Postal Station J. This was back in the 1990s. I sat near the window looking out at the alley, and when I lost my train of thought I listened to the letter carriers cheerfully insult each other. Whenever somebody came up with a really good line, all the carriers would let out a shout: "Woo, woo, woo, woo!"

One noon when I arrived at J to start work the shout greeted me even before I was in the door. There were three reasons for this: Mino Fuoco's wife had left him, he'd come back from the morning part of his walk drunk, and the other carriers were holding a party for him.

In the lunchroom big tinfoil trays of Chinese food covered the tables. And in the carriers' pleasure at being able to eat as much as they could stuff in, Mino and his grief were being ignored. Instead the carriers were gathered around Tommy Chu and young Dean Arlette.

Tommy and Dean were talking about babies.

Dean said, "The reason babies cry so much in the hᵣ can't cool down."

Tommy, who had three boys of his own, nodd

Dean leaned forward earnestly. "They can't sweat. You see what I mean?"

"I do."

"They don't have the glands for it. They haven't developed enough."

"No glands," Tommy said.

"That's right."

Tommy held up a finger. "Well, suppose you had a kid you nicknamed Eagle. Lively kid. And he becomes a teenager with pimples and the whole rest of it. You could say, 'The Eagle has glanded.'"

Dean looked at Tommy, bewildered. John Duguid sitting across from them shook his head.

Wang Hsu kept looking at the table. Then he looked at John. Then he lifted up from his seat and leaned slightly and produced a huge blast that sounded like a trumpet being blown through a cloth sack.

The sickening smell of old oil being stored behind a Chinese restaurant seeped into the lunch room.

Tommy stood up. "What a fucking stink."

"It is pretty bad," Wang said, and stood up.

Ray of Sunshine stood up. "Wang, I can smell it from here, you disgusting thing."

John Duguid backed away from the table. Something of the Glasgow docks lingered in his voice. "Damn it, Wang, that smells like shit."

Rearing up like this in their dark blue jackets and peaked caps they looked like Maoists. Mino, who was standing behind them with his face red with tears, stepped up to John and Wang and put his hands on their shoulders.

"You know what? You're my home. This is my home!"

I was sitting on the counter, next to the microwave. Tommy came over to warm up more food. Standing beside the machine waiting for his fried rice to finish, he whispered: "Woo, woo, woo, woo."

They read *Macleans* and Chinese comic books and big hard-over science fiction novels, and every weekday they read *The*

Province from first page to last, marking up the three copies the station received until by four in the afternoon when the last letter carrier had finally run out of gossip the newspapers were so dogeared and annotated they might have been shipped from the penitentiary in the Fraser Valley, Oakalla.

I wanted to go to graduate school. It was a mercenary move — I wanted a doctorate so I'd be in a position to quit the post office and teach in a college. (I had just finished — I was in my forties and it felt late in the day — earning an MA from Simon Fraser University in Burnaby, a small city that abuts East Vancouver.) Sitting in the lunch room, listening to the carriers, I would dream about it. How great it would be! How interesting my life would be once I had my teaching job and was out of the PO forever!

2

A few months later I enrolled at the University of British Columbia, considered to be BC's premier university, as a PhD student.

Alas, something I hadn't known when I entered UBC's English Department was that its social order depended on ass kissing. I had taken the freedom I'd had at Station J for granted, mainly because it was a freedom I'd had my entire adult life. I had done many things in the post office; but never had I had to kiss ass. When you were told to kiss ass in the post office (if, for instance, a supervisor didn't like the way you slouched as you sorted your mail) it was framed as a direct order: "Bruce, this is a direct order. I am asking you to get off that stool and sort standing." If you disobeyed the direct order you were marched out of the plant with a guard on either side of you.

This suited me. What I found at UBC, though, alienated me to the core. The professors seemed unaware of what lay outside their school. Most of them had been so poisoned by years of being in a position of authority compared to their students that they'd become childish; and petulance, small-mindedness and a barely repressed anger at other men's ideas and achievements were the order of the day.

But my months at UBC did have one good effect: some nights after class by the time I reached downtown on my bus, I was immersed in two ideas I'd been thinking about on and off for nearly a decade now. I looked out the bus window at the boarded-up Chinese restaurants that just a year ago had been so busy; I stared at the façades of Woodward's and Funky Winkerbean's; I watched the faces of the people getting on and off the bus, faces which in this part of town carried hints of Boston Bar and Spences Bridge, little towns in the BC Interior; and as I watched them hug and say hello, I thought they were people who knew each other, part of a community that stretched for hundreds of kilometres on both sides of the Coast Range, real and alive.

Yet nobody knew about them; nobody wrote or spoke about them. That was the thing – the untalked-about or unthought-about relationship between Vancouver and the BC Interior, between Vancouver and its past – that I'd first started considering one night in the downtown postal plant; it involved what I increasingly thought of as Vancouver's colonial culture, of which the English Department at UBC (and even more my reaction to that department) now seemed an especially bad example.

On the first part of my going-home bus ride, starting at Alma just past the campus, I stood in the aisle, gently jostled by satellite kids from all over Asia. Some of them wore upwards of a thousand dollars worth of clothes and many had little mascots of pink and blue plastic dangling from their backpacks. These coloured toys swung back and forth. I thought about my obsessions. And I kept placing my happy afternoons in Station J side by side with these faintly nightmarish evenings during which I worriedly bounced up and down the stairwell of the Buchanan Building where most of the English classes were held, wondering if I'd ever get the degree that would conduct me into another world.

3

But that was some months to come. For now, UBC and all it meant was a happy dream. And it was during this time of dreaming that I started to keep notes.

Reading over what I wrote then, I can see the dirt from my hands on the yellow pads of paper I wrote on, dirt that came from the filthy canvas bags I unloaded from the trucks, from the piles of mail and above all from the inky newsprint of the thousands of flyers — "householders," we called them — that I handed out to the carriers. And I can feel the odd, somehow suspended atmosphere of those days.

Sharon Esson and I had started publishing *The Vancouver Review*; and it was strange to be writing my notes and putting out a literary magazine when I was working as a mail handler. One evening a small crew from CBC-TV came by and made me manhandle a binnie of mail so the world could see what a literatus looked like pushing around letters; the rest of the station studiously ignored both me and them. Sometimes a letter carrier would shout: "Hey Bruce, what in the fuck are you tryin' to do here? I could build New York City with all these fucking householders! Take them away!" I'd shout back, "Take them away yourself! I'm gonna bury you!" And though this was feeble — I was never tough enough — carriers would shout, "Woo, woo, woo, woo!"

4

Often I made my notes after all the carriers had gone home. The station's quietness would seem enhanced by the slanting five o'clock sun. Ray Ling would be sitting in his office doing his paperwork. At the front counter Sam Wong and George Wong would be talking in sleepy voices about the houses they were getting built.

One especially quiet afternoon, like bubbles frothing up in their conversation, George let out a gurgling, high-pitched giggle. "I forgot to tell you! This guy come in this morning while you on your break. He had a hundred fuckin' boxes. He want me to wrap them all. Customers everywhere, lined up out the door. And he want me to stop everything. I say, 'Sir, you do it. You see I'm busy?' So he start shouting at me! Fuckin assho! I don't need to take shit like that! I say, 'You can't be civil mister, you get out! You get out!' I say. 'You can't be civil, you leave!' Fuckin assho! Ha ha! Fuckin assho!"

George's ecstatic giggle, a fountaining of delight, awoke my own sense of joy. I smiled and looked up. Dust motes in the air. The smell of burnt coffee. I put my pen down and lit a cigarette. The feeling of tranquillity edged with sadness that almost always took hold of me on those sunny late August afternoons now gave way to a happiness that made me restless.

"Hey Ray," I called, "I'm going out."

I slipped out the back, walked past the empty cages across the shadowy loading dock. Down the steps.

I headed down the alley. With its tall grasses growing out of the patched pavement, its quiet, its inky stripes of shadow, its empty lots full of shining weeds on my right and on my left, the block-long brick wall of the old Zeller's building warm with light, that alley entranced me. Using a black felt-tip pen, someone months or years before had written a high school graffito on the Zeller's wall:

E
VAN
S
T

RULES

Next to this graffito someone else had written — with a lipstick or red crayon, the thick line wavering on the brick and now faded almost to grey:

KATSYA
I LOVE

As I walked to my bank machine at Penticton and Hastings on that warm, sunlit afternoon I felt I was in the heart of the world. I felt — not at home, that was impossible for someone who'd moved as much as I had — but alert, alive, aware not just of the physical dimensions of the city around me, but also of the temporal dimension which the slanting afternoon sun seemed to embody.

That fall I would go to UBC — I wanted, so late in the day, to push the life I'd been born into behind me, push it all away. At the same time, as if I had a foreboding about my future at UBC (I would quit after one semester), those yellow notepads with the dirt on their pages that made my pen skip were filling up with descriptions and mini-essays that kept going back in time, as if it was in fact the old natal world that I was really interested in.

I had reached two paths. Down one path lay research, specialization, scholarship. Down the other lay the old world whose terminus was the letter carriers and "Woo, woo, woo." I should have known which one I would take. Already, while I was earning my MA up at SFU I had received a C- for an essay I had written on William Henry Drummond. C-, the lowest grade you can give a graduate student without failing him. The teacher said that I hadn't footnoted my essay according to PMLA standards. I asked her: Was there anything lacking in my writing? No; in fact, I wrote well, as she was sure I knew, but my carelessness with footnotes was unforgivable. In the end the head of the department – a woman whom I liked and who liked what I and my friends were doing with *The Vancouver Review* – walked up to me one day waving my record and said: "Bruce. Listen. This C- isn't acceptable. You have to kiss her ring. Call her up. Today. Apologize for not footnoting the piece properly and tell her you'll get it to her, properly footnoted, as soon as possible."

So I did.

Two paths, two ways of thinking about books and ideas and the world in which I lived. One day in the late nineties I went through all my yellow notepads. I began to rewrite them. In the process nearly every sentence changed, but that work of transformation produced most of the essays contained in this book.

The Secret

1

It was October. I had been living in North Vancouver for three months. And that morning when I walked to school, I was struck by the size of the leaves on the trees. They were like fairy tale leaves. Everything was outsized — huge: the trees that rose up into the sky, the leaves that hung from their branches. In that moist sunlight I picked a maple leaf one morning and wrapped it around my face. I thought: an elf could use this leaf like a boat. (North Vancouver was on the wet, bushy side of Burrard Inlet, right up against the Coast Mountains, and it was indeed like a temperate jungle compared to Vancouver.)

A few weeks later, coming home from school along the path, part of a flung-out string of kids, Brian Dooley from my class surprised me by running up and saying, "Hey, come on! Lonnie's gonna eat poo!"

Pleased to be invited but cautious, I followed him through thick bush into an open area by a powerline. The faint smell of gunpowder hung in the air. I could see exploded cylinders of red paper all over the ground, some of them strings of ladyfingers, some of them bombs thick as my wrist. Lonnie and a small kid with red cheeks sat on the chipped concrete block in which the hydro line was embedded. In his hand Lonnie was holding a piece of brown shit. His eyes were uncertain, like those of a boy getting ready to jump off the high diving board.

Brian said, "Okay, let's see you eat it."

"Okay."

Lonnie lifted the piece of shit to his lips and bit into it.

"Holy cow," Brian said. The small boy giggled and covered his mouth.

"Is that his poo?" I said.

"Yeah," Brian said.

We watched him eat it all.

"Okay," Brian said. "Now let's see you eat this spit bug." He pulled a leaf off a bush that had what looked to me like a big gob of saliva on it except that it was purer than spit, white and frothy.

Lonnie ate the spit bug.

2

So that was one thing. Then one day during gym, when we opened the doors and ran outside we entered another universe. Boys disappeared into it. Trees disappeared then loomed up in front of me. And in the fog I could hear seagulls and smell the salt air.

3

Fog, big leaves, Lonnie eating his own poo – and a dead bear in the rain, in a ditch just off the side of the road. Hundreds of little white worms were boiling up around the stick that a boy from my school was poking it with. These were maggots. The bulk and smell of the dead bear, and just a few feet into the bush a darkness almost as dark as night — it all gave me a strong sense of the oppressiveness and even danger of this new world I was in. In Hinton, Alberta, the small pulp mill town we had just come from, it had been different. The bush was open. Sunlight blazed in patches on the forest floor. It was easy as pie to step off the sidewalk into the forest.

One afternoon, while I was walking home from school, I started looking for a place where I could do just that. I couldn't find one. The bush was impenetrable.

I couldn't accept this. I walked and walked, trying to get to the end of the roads and houses. I was following old patterns; half-consciously I aimed for that point where I could step off the hard featureless sidewalk and slip into the forest's complexity. But no such point came.

Finally I hesitated. Where was I going? I stood there on the sidewalk. As far as I could see, the streets lined with lawns and houses continued. Sighing, I turned around and trudged back home.

4

I started grade seven in a new, bigger school. The kids seemed much older than I was. The girls wore lipstick. The boys dressed in jeans and snappy striped shirts. Me, I still wore elastic-waisted gabardine pants that were soiled in the front from my anxious fiddling with them.

I persuaded my parents to buy me some jeans, but I rarely went out. I stayed home after school, pacing the halls, looking at my new jeans in the mirror, reading and eating cereal at the kitchen table.

5

Then about a year and a half after we first moved to North Vancouver (and just before we moved again to Allenby Landing, another mill town, this one two ferries up the BC coast), I became friends with Sherman Leigh. He was in my class, a lanky, thoughtful boy who would sit on the floor with the bottom half of his legs turned out to the side.

One day in January we were sitting in his room tracing from a Camelot record jacket onto sheets of paper the Olde English letters of the word "Camelot." Both of us had become obsessed with the musical, and obsessed in particular with the way the romance of its story seemed to be physically embodied in the curlicues and ligatures of the old-style letters; now we had decided to make books that had the words of all the songs in them.

Sherman looked up.

"Can you ski?"

"Uh-huh."

"Want to go skiing with us?"

"Where're you going?"

"Mount Baker."

I skied well. In Hinton I could ski by the time I was six. But I didn't have the clothes that North Vancouver kids wore when they skied. In particular, I didn't have the stretch pants that were an essential part of the look.

That evening, keyed up, I asked my parents if they could buy me a pair.

"No."

"*Please.*"

"No!" My dad was angry. "We don't have the money for you to buy a pair of stretch ski pants for one trip to Mount Baker. Don't even think about it."

Furious at him, I went to my room. Then I remembered: my mom had stretch pants, black ones, with elastic straps that went under the foot so I could pull them up tight and give them the right look.

That night I tried them on. They came up to my chest.

"They're maybe a bit too big," my mom said.

"Can you fix them?"

"Fix them how?"

"I don't know. Maybe you could pin them or something. Or put a belt around them. Or something. I don't know!"

My mom set to work. Eventually, pulled up tight, folded in, pinned with safety pins to my shirt, and with a belt around them, they came up almost to my neck. But with my heaviest sweater over them, none of this showed.

The next day I clumped over to the Leighs' house in my old ski boots that almost didn't fit me any more. I was carrying my old

poles and my brown wooden skis with their old-fashioned bind-
ings. I pressed the doorbell; I heard it bong in the hallway. It was
raining hard, and my parka was wet. I could see how scratched
and old my skis were. But none of this mattered. I was wearing
black stretch pants pulled tight, and with my parka over my thick
blue sweater I looked passable.

Still, I worried. I was afraid I would overheat. So in the back-
seat of the car where I sat beside Sherman I kept the window
open a bit and didn't move.

At Baker we skied; and when it started to rain we went inside a
restaurant to get hot chocolate.

Warm from our exertions, we took off our parkas. I still had
my heavy sweater on, though, and the black stretch ski pants that
came up to my neck.

We sat and drank the chocolate. Sherman's dad kept looking
at me.

Finally he said, "Bruce, maybe you should take off your sweater.
You're dripping with sweat."

"I'm okay."

"You sure?"

"Oh yeah."

I smiled down at the table. As I did so, embarrassment at the
sweat running down my forehead made my neck and the sides
of my face flush. The heat of my embarrassment joined with
my body heat. Staring at the table, a doglike grin on my face, I
glowed red.

Then Sherman did something that wasn't like him. He smiled
and reached over and took hold of my sweater.

"Leave it alone!"

Glaring at him, I pulled the sweater down. I could feel the
sweat run down my forehead and cheeks, feel it slide down my
sides from my armpits. I was exquisitely aware of my mom's
pants that encased me, with their folds, their safety pins, the belt
cinched around their waist — pants like a kind of lurid feminine
skin nearly covering me.

Sherman reached for me again.

"Leave me alone!" I shouted.

6

Much later, when I started to write essays and reviews, I wrote like Walter Benjamin or Roland Barthes. I wonder, has anyone written about the really painful nakedness of one's first literary imitations, where any reader can see that you're trying to be someone else? In my case, when I look at old essays of mine I feel singed by the same flames of embarrassment I would have felt had Sherman seen my mom's ski pants, encasing me like a kind of second skin.

Yet I had to do it. Just as I'd seen something essentially glamorous in the way the skiers in North Vancouver dressed, something I had to copy, so a few years later it was essential that I make my sentences look the way the sentences looked in the works of the writers I admired.

All writers start like this. They imitate what they love. Then after a while the imitations give way to something which is their own.

But my situation was desperate. I was from the sticks. I had nothing to work with. No book I had ever read had said anything about Alberta pulp mill towns. The landscape hadn't been written about; and so – except in an intimate way that remained useless to me – it didn't exist. I found literary reality elsewhere, in books written in other countries. True, they fit me as awkwardly as my mom's ski pants had, but in the face of their glamour I had no choice: I had to imitate them.

That's what it means to be a colonial writer: a gap exists between who you are and who you want to be. Only slowly does that gap narrow; sometimes years have to pass before the person you are can speak and write. Sometimes that person remains mute.

Chinatown

1

When I was in my early twenties I lived alone, below Vancouver's Hastings Street, in an isolation so great it was like an ocean in which I swam far out and only then felt the currents that could pull me down. And without entirely knowing it I searched out people. I liked to shop either at Woodward's with the crowds or at the busy Orange Crush Market. Occasionally I'd go for tobacco to a Chinese grocery store down on Powell, close to the docks. And around this time I started getting my hair cut at Tom's.

I liked the atmosphere. I thought of Tom's as an outpost of the Orient, a small piece of Chinatown that had wandered off and settled down on East Hastings between a TV repair store and a corner grocery.

"You want your hair styled? You want a perm?"

"Just a cut, Tom, thanks."

I was unusual. All day long Chinese from the neighbourhood came into Tom's to get their hair done. Frowning young men sat with their heads leaned back over plastic bowls while Tom's assistants fingered their wet scalps. Then with curlers in their hair they read Chinese magazines that were both decorous and lurid. The air stank of hydrogen peroxide. Chinese music wailed. Red and yellow streamers of shiny metallic paper hung on the walls and gave the barbershop an air of downhome festivity. The customers lined up like patients in a doctor's office.

Tom said, "Why do you want to get your hair thinned?"

"So I can brush it. So it stays in place."

"You should get it styled, like me."

"If I had hair like yours I would get it styled." I waited a moment, then said, "I wanted to ask you about that. Why do these Chinese guys get their hair curled?"

"Simple. In China everyone has straight hair. Everyone. You get your hair curled you stand out. You look elegant man."

He turned my head, clipped with his comb and scissors. "Hey, you go to SFU?"

"Yeah."

"You in arts?"

"How'd you know?"

"You talk. Arts students talk. Guys in business and science, they don't talk. They're serious."

2

I was nineteen. Four months earlier I'd returned to Vancouver from three and a half years in Houston, Texas, and I still lived in a world where black men lowered their eyes to white teenagers and all night huge insects hung in shifting and rather monstrous globes of darkness around the lights at the gas station where I worked from eight at night to eight in the morning, seven days a week.

But here on the winter sidewalk at Main and Hastings I was in another country.

My breath exploded in the cold air. And maybe because of the cigarette laced with hashish that I'd smoked, I felt as if I'd entered an earlier century, a medieval time when lank-haired men and pigtailed Chinese and drunkards with the faces of gargoyles all congregated in the cold winter light.

Everything I saw looked as if it belonged in another century; and everything made me a little afraid. A bent-over woman slowly pulled a handmade wagon down the sidewalk. Two little kids sat in it, both of them calm and black-eyed as baby bears. My heart pounding with apprehension, I walked past an old woman with a witch's face out of a fairy tale who was taking tiny steps along the curb, so crippled she had to walk with one arm raised and with her head turned upward staring at the sky.

It started to rain. I felt the chill of it on my face. I decided to go to a restaurant I'd heard of. Pamela, my old girlfriend before I'd gone to Houston, had mentioned it. She told me she often ate at the Ho. Maybe I'd see her there. I hoped so. Uneasy as I felt, it would be good to have company. I said to a vendor, "Do you know where the Ho Cafe is?"

"Not here!" Two of his teeth were black.

"Could you tell me where?"

He kept working. I stayed where I was, not knowing what else to do. Red and blue and yellow rain fell in the store lights and threw streaks of colour into the street.

Then the vendor stepped onto the sidewalk. He put his hand lightly on my shoulder. He pointed in the rain that had now started to come down hard.

"Cross the street. Go till you see an alley. On your right. Go down the alley. You see it!"

In the freezing rain, shaking from the cold, my heart beating with fright, I ran past mounded-up piles of wet cardboard. Even in the cold the alley stank of something dreadful. Rain glittered in the streetlights like white rice. I saw the door of the cafe. Heart hammering, I went inside.

Formica kitchen tables. Fluorescent light. Blue flames hissing under steaming pots. I noticed the swirls of dirt that a mop had made on the linoleum floor. In its bareness and dinginess, it was like no cafe I'd ever been in. A woman standing at the grill shouted at me in harsh Chinese, and nearly fainting at the strangeness of it all I shouted back: "Hello! I'm Canadian too!"

3

One day in spring after weeks of rain the sun came out and I went walking up Clark Drive, then west through Strathcona.

Because it hadn't been sunny for so long the plants were pent up. All along the street pine cones popped open in the warm sun with the sound of a person softly snapping his fingers.

But as I entered Chinatown it began to cloud up and darken. By the time I hit Pender Street, it was cold again and raining hard.

I looked in the window of a cafe. Men sat at the long counter, a few of them dressed in old suits. I liked the way they looked. I went inside and took a seat at the counter and tried to imitate the men's demeanour.

But to do that I needed to relax. That was the secret. I'd worked in the BC Interior for two summers, and in each town I'd stayed at there'd been a Chinese cafe I could go into out of the hot afternoon, tired and at ease, watching whomever came in the door with lighthearted interest. But it was different here and I couldn't find that lightheartedness in me. I was in China-town, not on a gravel street lined with trucks, with cottonwood seed blowing in the air and the early willow leaves falling into the river just a few hundred yards away.

The counter faced a wall lined with old mirrored tiles that had discoloured so that looking at your reflection was like looking at a drowned man staring up at you out of dark water. A calendar showed a red-cheeked Peking opera singer. Cups in their saucers sat balanced three high in neat rows. With the rain falling hard outside, the cafe seemed like a cave cored out of the old build-ing and the men themselves seemed like visitants from an earlier time, figures from old railroad shacks and plywood cafes come down to the coast.

The proprietor placed my coffee in front of me. I rolled a ciga-rette, and the man sitting to my right watched with interest. He had a delicate, highcheeked face and eyes as gentle as a poet's. When the proprietor's back was turned he slipped a bottle of Five Star out of his suitcoat and unscrewed it and put some of the whiskey in his coffee.

"You want?" he whispered.

"Why not."

"Make your hot go."

He winked.

I winked back and rolled a cigarette for him. He accepted it with pleasure. We smoked and drank the coffee and whiskey and watched the proprietor carefully mix crushed egg shells in with the coffee, then put the mixture into the pot to be perked.

Then in the booth behind us two people started to argue. They were a man and a woman.

"I love you. Don't you understand that?"

"Oh, fuck."

"Don't swear at me like that."

"Don't swear at me like that," he mocked her.

"You asshole."

"You asshole."

"Billy, stop this, please." Now she was crying.

I turned on my stool. The man had gotten up from the bench seat and stood by the table. A Native man. He wore a T-shirt and jeans and he was tall and well built, with long hair and an impassive face.

"Don't leave me," she pleaded.

She stood up from the bench seat and moved towards him and tried to put her arms around his waist. And now I realized they were drunk. He moved back and she fell out of the bench seat of the booth onto the floor.

"Fuck, look at you."

The man stepped back. Crying, her nose running, she started to crawl on the floor towards him.

"Please Billy. Please."

"Fuck you're disgusting. Get away from me."

I sat motionless. The Chinese men in the cafe watched somberly. I got ready to move from my stool. Then the proprietor stood beside the man, his hand on his shoulder.

"Maybe you go now," he said.

The man batted at the hand. But he moved away a few feet and the proprietor carefully lifted up the crying woman. "Come, you sit here," he said and led her to a booth at the back. The man stood near the door watching. Then he went outside into the rain.

With the rest I turned back on my seat and smoked and drank my coffee and thought about how the proprietor had acted. A memory came to me. The spring before I'd been deadheading with a Canadian Pacific steel gang known as the Mission Boys, and that hot May afternoon we'd stopped near Three Valley Gap to pick up some equipment. The Shuswap was in flood and swallows swooped ecstatically inches from the water. It was a beautiful day. I'd been tanning on the roof of one of the bunk cars, reading Solzhenitsyn's *The First Circle* and watching the leaves in a nearby aspen grove glitter and tremble. Then someone noticed the graves. They were in tall grass near the white-capped river, not far from the tracks. A few sticks with Chinese characters on them, bleached by the sun nearly to invisibility. I'd jumped down to look, pushed more by joy at being alive than by curiosity.

But handling the sticks had felt strange.

"They're old," I said.

Duck, one of the Mission Boys, squatting nearby on his cowboy boots, said, "Fucking right."

Four or five of us stood or squatted there in the sun, looking at the sticks. The oldest maybe twenty-three.

I drank my coffee now with the rain falling outside. How had those Chinese men felt, squatting like Duck in the night where a resort complex was now, smoking and ki-yiing to each other or listening to the river make its hushing noise? How had they died? Cholera? Influenza? Overwork? Some must have died of unhappiness. And some must have fallen soundlessly into canyons that were like the canyons in pictures of old China. Now they were ghosts, and these men in the cafe were their descendants.

A Chest of Drawers

1

I returned to Vancouver from Texas with my girlfriend Cate when I was nineteen. And for a long time I went almost every week to the old public library down on Robson Street.

That library is long gone now. But in those days it became my second home. I was very young, younger than my years, and for me the library was an atmospheric place, as full of Cate as a house is full of the smell of a smashed bottle of perfume. Before we broke up, she had often gone there with me, so that if I saw a girl with narrow shoulders and thick heavy hair between the rows of books my heart would pound. And because I was only nineteen and in many ways innocent, it was erotic in another way with its mezzanine washroom that stank of piss and the mixed sweat and shit smell of the old men who stood beside you jerking their wattled cocks as you peed.

After Cate moved out of the basement suite we'd shared for a year I got a second-storey room in an old house on Broadway near the BOW-MAC sign, Bowell-Maclean Motors' lurid masterpiece, at that time probably the biggest piece of neon in Vancouver. You reached my room up a steep flight of unpainted plywood stairs that had no bannister and really wasn't much more than a ladder. A twenty-watt bulb hung in the hallway's murk (I can still smell the cat piss impregnated in the hallway

22

carpet when I think of that murk), and the door to my room was painted the same chocolate brown as the doors to the other three rooms. It was from that room that I'd emerge to go to the library. I read my first Canlit here: David Fennario's *Without a Parachute* (every day I heard voices on the street that sounded like the voices in the pages of his little book) and the great poems of Margaret Avison. And one day, sitting at one of the long tables on the third floor, I started reading Michel Tremblay's play *Les belles soeurs*.

I was stunned by it. Never before had I encountered characters who wanted so much to touch those they were speaking to. Hand-gestures accompanied their talk, arm-grabbings. It was as if the world from which I had only recently emerged — a pulpmill town world of screaming kids and kitchen floors dirty with Cheerios and gobs of sticky jam, a world in which my Polish dad and French-Canadian mom shouted ethnic insults at each other (they had an intense sexual love, my parents, but they were desperate, up against the wall, bitterly unhappy) — it was as if this world had been presented with all of its atmosphere intact. Just as in my family, the changes of fortune that again and again overcame Tremblay's people went hand in hand with a tendency towards unabashed display, theatricality for the sake of theatricality. They cried, screamed, tore each other apart in arias of language that at times rose to the pitch of violence. Each of the characters was sharply presented. But since they were constantly interacting with each other, the strongest impression I got wasn't of any one individual; the strongest impression I got was of the loud, intense domesticity of a Catholic milieu.

Oh, that domestic Catholicism! I grew up with it; and like the incense at midnight mass that when I get a headache I can still smell, I would recognize it anywhere. When I read Tremblay's play (and after *Les belles soeurs* I read all his plays, one after the other) I was still close to the street, only recently off welfare, ravaged by anxiety, half-drowning in my family and trying desperately to reach dry ground. And sometimes reading one or another play — *En pièces détachées*, for instance: "And you think you weren't cheap, you of all people! When you'd come in at four

in the morning and wake all the neighbours up yelling and singing and swearing, and you think that wasn't being cheap?! And
then you go and have the gall to talk to me about Claude! To
blame me for making him the way he is today when you know
very well he came into the world like that and the doctor told
us he'd never have the mind of any more than a four-year-old
boy. Do you remember what he looked like when he was first
born, Helene? Do you remember? Tell me you remember how he
looked! Tell me, Helene! Tell me!" — sometimes, reading one of
these plays, I had to get up from the table.

Because I recognized everything. The coarseness, the anger,
the self-pity, and especially the violent, unabashed, almost
childlike speech — all this I knew. I was immersed in familiarity. I could hear the screaming fights, sickening with self-hatred
("Polish pig!" "French cow!"), and I could smell the baloney
cupping up in the frying pan and see the black cracks in the
linoleum floor. It was the first time that the language I thought of
as Canadian had appeared before me in print. As I read I heard
my mom's and aunts' jokes, and also a quality in their voices, in
their way of making words: a vehemence that was lyrical and
"confused" and had the full weight of their bodies behind it.
Presented with genius, it was a vehemence that summed up my
childhood.

2

Many years later, in the early eighties, while I was still working
in the downtown postal plant I started reading Michel Tremblay's *The Fat Woman Next Door is Pregnant*, the opening volume of his great sequence of books *Les Chroniques du plateau
Mont-Royal*.

Almost from the first page I was taken back to that earlier reading. Like the stories us postal clerks would tell as we sat side by
side sorting on the forward primary, *The Fat Woman* was about
a place, first of all — the area around la rue Fabre in East Montreal — and the dozens of people associated with that place, especially little Marcel and his sister Therese and the other members

of three families who lived on top of each other in an old house on la rue Fabre.

But it wasn't this huge crowd of characters — all of them vivid — that startled me. What startled me was this: Though Tremblay was writing about a city thousands of miles away, so closely did his storytelling methods resemble those that entranced me during our nights sorting, so homely and familiar was the book's feeling, that as I read it I seemed to see section after section of the old Vancouver that for me the postal plant had long since come to represent. And like those folded paper cities that pop up when you open the pages of certain children's books, as I read there appeared before me the projects near the Hastings Viaduct where Ann Jack lived with the son who had punched her in the face, the old stucco houses on Glen Drive that I passed when I went to visit Toni Leigh, George Vincent's gloomy hole on Lakewood full of copies of *Vogue* magazine, Jen's apartment up on Graveley where her mom made her pancakes when she came home from work and finally, connecting all these places, the city I saw when I pedalled home from the plant down Hastings and Powell: the Woodbine Hotel, the bus wires overhead, the wet skies and the North Shore mountains.

A magical effect. It was due in part to the fact that *The Fat Woman* was the first of the *Chroniques*. It introduced everyone, set the stage for what was to come. And so just as in the post office when we would start one of our stories by naming the characters who would appear on the Ed Sullivan show, trying not to miss a single one, so *The Fat Woman* ended up being an extended and loving act of naming. Everything in it took place on one day — May 2, 1942, the "first day of spring" in Montreal — and as I read the book it soon came to resemble the chest of drawers in Marcel's house that so fascinates him:

> Like the other children he had been told that they had all been found in various drawers the day that they were born: at the very top were the twin drawers of Therese and Richard, bigger than the others and blacker too; then came those of Phillipe and Marcel, wedged into the inter-

lacings of carved wood; and finally, a little lower still, the one for the baby to come. It was tiny, a glove drawer in fact, plain, somewhat lost. Marcel would often be seen gazing at this secret drawer. He didn't dare to touch it and if anyone asked what he was doing there, he said: "I'm waiting for the mail!"

The Fat Woman resembled this chest of drawers especially in its structure. The book is short, and it contains approximately 75 chapters; and though I went from one chapter to the next in the order dictated by the pagination, I felt strongly that they all had a simultaneous existence, a sense which was due to the fact that Tremblay wandered from house to house — proceeded digressively, that is, just as we'd do in the post office ("Another time when we were watching TV at my friend Eddie's place –") instead of going from day to day.

And something else made me think about that chest of drawers. Each drawer (each chapter) contained a scene. Start a new chapter — Bam! there you were! Two or three or four human beings shouting at each other, crying, telling a story, berating someone or just opening a window onto the new spring world. So much was this the case that I experienced the same magic that Marcel felt: a miniaturized world, a whole heap of human beings, seemed to pop out at me as one drawer after another was opened.

3

Then there was the second book in the series, *Therese and Pierrette and the Little Hanging Angel*. Again and again in that book Tremblay spilled out a cornucopia that reminded me of old places and times, in particular a stretch of Victoria Drive in East Vancouver where a Bingo hall used to stand just across from the playground of a Catholic school. Radio shows, escapist novels, people lying in bed in the middle of the afternoon, the ghost of a dead cat named Duplessis, screaming mothers, three Fates who sit on a porch knitting, a farting nun, a monstrous Mother Superior, love affairs, sex jokes, a little girl who hangs in the air in a Catholic pageant, a transvestite, and a young man who gets a hardon every time he looks at Therese — this was just some of what I found in the book.

So much there! And all of it had a specific atmosphere — an atmosphere that made me think of junior high dances, with their balloons and patent leather shoes, their red faces and sweaty hands. When I read *The Fat Woman* and *Therese and Pierrette*, in fact, and absorbed their ecstatic and painful atmosphere, it so impressed me that I concluded that nothing like these books existed in English-Canadian fiction. But what was it that so fundamentally distinguished them? It took me awhile; then I realized the books were vulgar — a more radical and more complicated fact than it might seem.

"Vulgar" comes from a Latin word meaning "of the people." But English Canadian writing is almost never "of the people," even linguistically. (Think of the difference between most Canadian novels and *Trailer Park Boys*.) And one of the most important consequences of this fact is that with few exceptions it describes a sober world that emphasizes what is final in people's lives. It is concerned with fates. It is therefore basically tragic.

Tremblay's books, on the other hand — precisely because they are vulgar — inhabit a comic universe, revealing on almost every page that delight in the childish, the outrageous, the suddenly-occurring (Kramer pops through the door!) which you see every night on sitcoms and which is at the heart of popular culture.

Don't misunderstand me: the Montreal working-class parish Tremblay writes about is a rough place. But just as in the post office I would hear stories about miscarriages and husband troubles mixed in with the most chatty reminiscence, so in Tremblay's books even terrible events seemed to be part of the old slow course of the world. When Albertine, for instance, screamed out her hatred of sex to her sister, or Marie-Louise became paralyzed with fear about the baby growing in her, I didn't feel (as I would have with most Anglophone fiction) that I was witnessing someone's fate; instead I felt that these miseries were just one part of life, which the next moment might include a sequence of contentment and even joy.

But this only partly explains what makes Tremblay's novels so unlike most Canadian texts. Along with this, along with the delight found in the lurid and the fantastic, along with the homely knowledge that life goes on no matter what, Tremblay adds the intoxication of colloquial speech at its most unbuttoned. His women in particular intoxicated me: in the least inflection of their voices I caught a trace of the tight girdles and *moitse mon Chriss* vehemence I had known as a boy. Like some future fly on the wall, I couldn't stop reveling in these women's screaming, embarrassed delight in "the dirty." All of them (and this is something they share with the characters of other great popular artists, from Richard Pryor to Lucille Ball) had something of the child in them. In the mental atmosphere of their speech and the way they reacted with each other, I got the same sense of impressions crowding in that you get with children, and also the sudden shifts in mood — the casual malice, for instance, that can all at once turn to tenderness, or that sudden moral vehemence that children, who feel things so strongly, are sometimes able to command. Listen for instance to Charlotte Cote, the mother of the "little hanging angel" Simone in *Therese and Pierrette*, finally turning all her childhood pain and fear at the hands of sadistic nuns into a "ribbon of endless phrases" directed at the monstrous Mother Benoite, who has been about to treat Simone exactly as Charlotte herself was treated:

> Aren't you ashamed! Doesn't it ever get to you, being so mean! When you go to bed at night and think over what you've done that day, the way you nuns always taught us to do, don't you blush with shame? Don't you turn blue with shame? All the punishments you've handed out and all the times you humiliated us, don't they choke you? Nothing's changed here. You still take out your frustrations on poor defenceless kids who trust you to show them how to live their lives! You've always got a crucifix in one hand and a

wooden ruler in the other! As long as we're on that subject, why don't you just light out at the kids with the crucifix in both hands — it'd hurt them more! Is it because you just haven't got that far yet, or is your hypocrisy holding you back? I spent seven years here, not all that long ago, and what I remember about it isn't very happy. Childhood ought to be a happy time, but my memories of the time I spent here are rotten and dirty and twisted because of crazy women like you who don't know the first thing about children.

It goes on and on, for two and a half pages. Tremblay can't resist this kind of thing. But then neither can his audience; shocking and even hurtful though this attack on the church might be to them (and part of Tremblay's allure has always been his power to shock), it is theirs, this vehemence, the exact tone of voice that they would use in similar circumstances. Even in translation it isn't a voice I have ever heard in English-Canadian fiction. It comes from a different world — a world of silenced husbands and ignorant and vehement wives, a world where cramped frustration is mixed up with a sickly-sweet Catholicism and where people don't talk in polished sentences but kiss, shout, expostulate, and scream with an anger that after many decades still rings in my ears.

Wearing a Mask

1

While I was working on Vancouver Island near Port Hardy my best friend Alistair died. And with that, at least for me, the hippie era came to an end.

When I returned to Vancouver I got a job as a janitor on the night shift. The job suited me. It gave me a world that was complete in itself. I could work all night riding the big waxers and buffers through the halls, come home, read for half an hour, sleep through the day, go to work again. I made friends with an East Indian janitor named Dhillon, and through him I met a young woman, Leila, an office cleaner, who let me pull her pants down and finger her and even take her a few times into the closets.

The building I lived in was on Powell Street, one of a dozen or more that stretched like wet laundry along the docks — rain-stained stucco apartment blocks where women in T-shirts watched TV all day in units that stank of stale ashtrays and semen.

The building boiled with life. Hetty the manager — a tiny woman with bright blue eyes — had had a restraining order put on her husband and everyone talked about what a prick he was. Almost every day the Trovatis below me fought so loudly I could hear them even with my radio playing. My next-door neighbour Mary Willoughby went to the Princeton regularly with her boyfriend, and on my nights off I would stay up for them because a couple of times they'd come home drunk and I'd listened dry-mouthed on the other side of my door as they fucked standing up in the hall. The train thundered by at 1:45 AM, and in the early morning seagulls barked and screamed, eating the grain that had fallen on the tracks. Sparrows rested on the balconies and kids played in the street.

Most of the time I was part of all this. Winter gave way to spring; and in the possessive, unreasonable way of someone who all through his childhood and adolescence had moved I started to feel like I'd found a home. When I walked down Powell to Gas-town in the late spring evenings the white and grey and darker grey sky overhead and the dirty sidewalks littered with smashed whiskey bottles and soggy pieces of hot dogs sometimes seemed to belong to a city in a dream, so little had any of it changed in all the years I'd intermittently lived in Vancouver. But at other times this sense that I inhabited a dream world would be replaced by a truer insight; then my poverty, my isolation and a really fright-ening awareness of how quickly time was flying by would prod-uce in me a terror that when it passed left me numb.

I knew I should quit my job. But uncertainty gripped me. It was hard to let go of Leila and the security of the routine. It was even harder to let go of the paycheque. But then in July I did quit. I gave notice (so an old, folded sheet of paper tells me) on July 11, 1973. Friday, July 25 was my last day. The next day, Sat-urday, I dozed on and off all afternoon. Around two AM I fell asleep. When I woke the next morning at seven, too excited to sleep in, I had coffee and full of an almost giddy happiness I went out for a walk. And there I discovered a world as transformed as the world in the movie *Dark City* when at the end the door finally opens onto blue sky.

I found it was summertime: black shadows striped the side-walk and tall grasses grew against the corrugated metal walls of the old warehouses. A couple of Chinese boys out fishing sat on the railroad tracks with their knees up by their ears, fixing their rods. After being on graveyard for nine months, the warm sum-mer sun intoxicated me. I loved the soft air on my face. I loved the bright colours, the leaves on the trees, the birds singing, the colour of the bricks in the old brick buildings. I headed out to the docks and looked with joy at the shapes of the grain elevators, the railroad tracks shining in the strong morning light.

Later, walking home down Powell I passed a pretty Native prostitute who couldn't have been more than fifteen standing with one sandalled foot jacked back against the brick of the Princeton Hotel. She wore a short orange minidress that set off her brown legs and warm brown eyes. Smiling, she squinted against the sun. When she moved her foot along the wall, a delicate charm bracelet slipped around her ankle.

"Want some company?" she said.

"I don't know." I felt embarrassed. "Maybe I could take you out to coffee."

"Coffee!" She laughed. "You wanna buy me a ten-buck coffee, sure."

"Well, no, probably not," I said. "Not this morning."

"Too bad."

"You're awfully pretty, though," I said.

"Well, thaaaank you." Her sarcasm didn't cover up her happiness at being flattered.

A few mornings later — still intoxicated, as I headed up to the Kootenay Loop, with the heat and light of summer — I caught the 135 SFU bus up Burnaby Mountain and started my new life.

2

I was twenty-two, immersed in my student work, intensely happy — intoxicated by the university library's smell, even — and battling with an essay on Daniel Defoe's *Robinson Crusoe* when I started to read Roland Barthes. Right away I learned something interesting — Barthes sounded just like Defoe's hero. Wherever I turned in either Crusoe or Barthes I saw that the sentences ran to enormous lengths, held together by colons, semi-colons, and other signs of equivalence. I'd open Defoe at random, and here was Crusoe beginning his conquest of the island, discovering that the goats on the island were "so subtile, and so swift of foot, that it was the difficultest thing in the world to come at them":

> But I was not discouraged at this, not doubting but I might now and then shoot one; as it soon happened, for after I had found their haunts a little, I laid wait in this manner for them: I observed if they saw me in the valleyes, tho' they were upon the rocks, they would run away as in a terrible fright; but if they were feeding in the valleys, and I was upon the rocks, they took no notice of me; from whence I concluded that by the position of their opticks, their sight was so directed downward, that they did not readily see objects that were above them; so afterward I took this method, I always climbed the rocks first to get above them, and then had frequently a fair mark.

As a boy of ten or eleven, I had devoured Crusoe's efforts to domesticate his island. Now, reading *Robinson Crusoe* again, I immediately recognized in Defoe's huge sentences the faith in effort that had so won me over when I was small. I realized that just as Barthes did, Crusoe gave the reader a powerful image of *work*. Crusoe's gigantic sentences were a sort of unending activity of analysis that exactly corresponded to his original unending activity on the island. The lengths they ran to were possessive lengths: they demonstrated the great effort of the narrator to represent or recapture the initial physical and mental effort of which they spoke. Each of the sentences was like a job done, a piece of work finished; no facet of a sentence's original intention was left untouched, and both Crusoe and I seemed to arrive at the period with the same slightly exhausted satisfaction.

I loved that. And I felt the same love reading Barthes. In *Critical Essays* (a book I took out over and over again from the SFU library and eventually stole, shoving the book inside my shirt and partway into my jeans, then doing up my coat and glancing as I went out at the check-out clerk with the inquisitive eyes of a GP) I placed a tiny pencilled check beside the following sentence, which was typical of his work:

According to the third type of relation, the sign is no longer
situated with regard to its (virtual) "brothers," but with
regard to its (actual) "neighbours": in homo homini lupus,
lupus maintains certain connections with homo and with
homini; in garment systems, the elements of an outfit are
associated according to certain rules: to wear a sweater and
a leather jacket is to create, between these two garments, a
temporary but signifying association, analogous to the one
uniting the words of a sentence; this level of association is
the level of the syntagm, and we shall call the third relation
the syntagmatic relation.

The interlocking syntax of this writing, combined with the
tenacious way it moved over the most minute phenomena,
enthralled me. Barthes sounded more academic than Crusoe,
more impersonal; but in his writing I found the same continual
sense of work being done and that same surge of triumph at the
sentence's end.

And another great thing reminded me of Crusoe: none of
Barthes's writing *disturbed* me. Because someone had recom-
mended it I'd take a book out of the library; but when I discovered it contained stories about "real life," or dealt naturalistically
with family pain, I'd snap it shut. I hated that. I didn't want it.
I couldn't read it. And part of what I liked about the books of
Barthes and Defoe was that they didn't contain it.

To pick just one example, even though he was isolated on his
island for most of the book, there was no *loneliness* in Crusoe.
And so the great novel calmed me. Lying on my bed in my dark
little room I could read Defoe's book and feel immersed in a day-
lit atmosphere suffused with clarity and faith in human effort.

And it was the same with Barthes. Because his "I," so completely turned outward, never marked the inner anxiety of an
individual, it didn't awaken my own anxiety. Instead I turned to
Barthes for the same reason I turned to *Scientific American* and
The New Yorker (and Crusoe, too, of course) — for a powerful
feeling of order, a domestication of the world, a kind of cosiness.
The very assertiveness of Defoe's and Barthes's prose — the way

it worked, explained, categorized, summed up — made it comforting to read. It made the world "small," or at least not mysterious and unknowable. It told me that the world could be ordered, that a person, using his intelligence, could walk the length and breadth of his island and bring it under control.

And then it happened. Like one of those cartoon light bulbs going off, one day while I was reading the final long essay in Barthes's *Mythologies*, the idea of an urban Robinson Crusoe popped into my head. I thought: I can be that. From that day on, everywhere I turned in Barthes I found traces of this idea. In all his books now — *Mythologies*, *Critical Essays*, *Elements of Semiology*, *The Fashion System* — Barthes seemed to me to function as a sort of surveyor or mapmaker, brilliantly constructing his universe from the material finitude of forms. Everywhere in these books I found a Crusoe-like confidence and energy turned on the twentieth-century urban world: its buildings, texts, advertisements, photographs, movies, myths.

3

All this hugely appealed to me. But the appeal would have been less if Barthes hadn't been able to add something new, to find a modern equivalent for that strenuous, concrete prose that had gripped me since childhood in Defoe's book. The mapmaker or surveyor mentality was important; but what immediately infatuated me in Barthes was his verbal brilliance, the amazing contemporaneity of his language. To read him was to hear the modern world (or at least one aspect of it). It was to get a feeling of "the now" that was due more than anything else to Barthes's quasi-scientific yet somehow poetic vocabulary.

Ever since I'd been a kid drawing rocket ships on the brown kraft paper covers of my textbooks, I'd known that the language I used contained words that were like nothing that had come before them. *Computer, analogue, transistor, liquid fuel, atomic, cellular, switch on* — you just had to list a few of these words to get their flavour. They shared attributes: they had a scientific or technological feel; they lacked any sense of moral evaluation;

they implied complex functions or activities; and they sounded new.

New. When I looked at Barthes's characteristic vocabulary, that was exactly the quality I found there as well. Words like *paradigm, syntagm, diachronic,* and *polysemous plenitude* all irresistably suggested a kind of hyper-contemporary, even science-fiction-like take on the world. When I read Barthes on the grammar of movies, say, or on metonymy in Balzac, I stepped five minutes into the future.

Why did this matter so much? Why did such an allure attach to vocabulary? I can only say that for me his vocabulary made Barthes *popular,* in a strict sense of the word. His writing thrilled me, that is, in exactly the way I'd been thrilled all my life by other products of popular culture, with its constant upwelling of new things.

As a boy I'd read fairy tales, then gone straight to science fiction; and in each case what had sent me burrowing greedily through the books was the powerful sense of the strange and unprecedented that the stories evoked. I responded so strongly, in other words, because these stories were so in synch with the culture that produced them. Enchanted rings, castles beyond the north pole, robots, interstellar travel, positron drives, the crystal ball (what novel was it in?) that contained a simulacrum of the universe — fictional objects like this were completely in harmony with the unending stream of wonderful new things that the culture I lived in made available to me.

Even in Hinton, Alberta, the bush town I'd lived in from the ages of 5 to 10 (until I left home at 19, the longest I lived anywhere), even in Hinton each season brought something new. I was ravished in turn by glowing Viewmaster slides of Cinderella and her pumpkin coach, by the school scribblers that showed up in the drug store one year with their shiny purple and green covers in which moiré patterns appeared, and by the bags of marbles that one spring had two helixes of colour in them instead of the usual single twist of red or green or blue. And — jumping ahead a bit — I remember the thrill, almost the shock, of seeing the ordinary comic book panel I'd grown up with transformed in the sixties into a galaxy-spanning two-page spread in the middle of one of the first issues of *Doctor Strange.*

And Barthes's space-age writing continued that. Reading him was like hearing Bob Dylan's "Desolation Row" for the first time; it was like first seeing Honda's great science fiction movie *The Mysterians.* That intoxicating, fairytale newness which is so central to popular culture trembled in Barthes's 21st-century sentences the way it had trembled in some of the shots in Honda's film. I didn't think about it at the time, but it now seems to me no accident that his books were (and are) almost entirely read in the academy — an environment whose members are mostly young people. We were responsive.

And not just to Barthes. It thrilled me and my friends Paul and Rufus to first encounter those writers who were at the intellectual edge of the day — Heidegger, Merleau-Ponty, Foucault, Eco, Derrida and Lévi-Strauss, to name just a few. Little in the world excited us as much as the new thing their books embodied; it was like a stunningly powerful machine you could use to discuss anything. And it was beautiful: the language of the texts (which was nearly always translated), with its exotic, on-rushing syntax and science-fiction lexicon seemed brilliantly contemporary, and instantly made more familiar forms of writing appear stale.

Best of all you could put on this writing like a mask. How much cooler these authors were than people like Hardy or Chekhov whose writing you couldn't use because it depended on a knowledge of life! Just as we could wear dress shirts and pressed jeans to give ourselves a sharp, impassive appearance, so in our written texts we could use the syntax and vocabulary of these great intimidators to appear commanding and to demonstrate a decisive grasp of the issues.

And for me Barthes's prose especially hit the spot. Mimicking its baroque lexicon I could bypass my limited experience (I could be a "scientist of language"). Mimicking its quarter-page-long sentences I could feel powerful, in charge of what I faced. Writing à la Barthes gave me control: it gave me a way to be masterful and tough — a way of fiercely engaging a complicated world that had so far shrugged me off. If Barthes could be a Crusoe of the urban world, well, so could I! And so throughout my early twenties I attempted to write (or thought about writing, or talked about writing) essays on *The Buzzer* (a little pamphlet put out by BC Hydro that you can still find on Vancouver's buses), on the big wall murals in the Egmont Hotel where we used to go drinking, on *Alice in Wonderland* and even on suburban homes and their furnishings.

As it turned out, none of these essays were finished. Experience got in the way.

I wanted to be a writer. I had no time for secure academics. But as I would discover, neither finally did Barthes. As the years passed, and the seventies ended, he became ever more openly "insecure," increasingly eager to admit to a vision more personal than his work had so far allowed. He wanted to write a novel; he wanted to "speak his soul."

Yet how could he? All his life, as a Parisian intellectual, he had been surrounded by authoritative voices and had felt their pressure; and for a long time he had himself been an authority. And finally the temptations of the public voice were overwhelming. In the end all he could do was subvert that voice.

It wasn't enough. In *Crusoe*, you remember, Friday appears — terrified Friday, quaking before the white man — and with his appearance Crusoe becomes human (jealous of Friday, angry towards him, and finally tender and remorseful in one great scene), and the novel becomes immortal. For Barthes, though, as for all the Parisian *maitres*, there was no Friday, and so no story: he couldn't cross over into the promised land of fiction. But his efforts to do so were great; he tried hard. And because he tried so hard, a lot of this remarkable person got into his last books.

I still read him, impressed more than ever by his achievement. And when I read him it isn't just the books that grip me. I'm also held by what I see on the other side of the books — the image of what it was like to read him when I was young. Youth, they say, is unhappy because it has no voice of its own and so no way to express its experience. Certainly that was true for my friends and me in 1970s Vancouver. In that colonial town with its beer parlours and dirty sidewalks, we needed desperately to come to grips with the ideas we had discovered. Above all we needed a mask that we could speak through. For a short time Barthes gave me that mask — a voice, a style, a stance, a way to talk back to the world.

In fact, when I was reading him I started to become a writer – or at least I found a way to write that gave me access to my own world. Following Barthes's 1975 book *Roland Barthes* I started to take photographs and join them with short pieces of writing that were meant to float free of the pictures, to work less as captions than as miniature commentaries, little essays on what the pictures were about.

During those long summer evenings I photographed the other tenants in my apartment block. I photographed the docks, the railroad tracks. I photographed the young Native prostitute down by the Princeton Hotel, a startled look on her face, her black hair falling in her eyes.

"You weren't smiling," I said after I took the picture.

"Well, take another picture then."

I did. Twice I photographed her smiling; then less than a month later she was murdered. One day I watched as a short young Native man taped a picture of the girl to the alley wall at Powell and Semlin where her body had been dumped. Above the picture he wrote with a black felt tip pen:

Eleanor Mearns
Left this Cold City
On August 22, 1975.

I watched him work. One of his arms was bandaged to the elbow with a dirty bandage that was coming undone. And one of his front teeth stuck over his lower lip. I said: "Did you know her?"

"My sister." He looked at me with eyes that were as brown and warm as hers had been. "You know her?"

I shook my head. "No."

He nodded. "Well, someone knew her. Enough to kill her." He smiled, as if he had made a joke.

"I guess you could put it that way," I said.

"It's true, isn't it? Someone knew her enough to kill her." And again he smiled.

He took a last look at his work; then he walked away. And that too I see — an image of shame, one of those youthful moments that becomes reduced — simpler and smaller and almost empty of meaning as time passes — that too I see when I go through my Roland Barthes books.

Stardust

1

Pamela had a chunky body; she wore black knee-high boots and black stockings and black and white nubbly skirts over shirts that lacked sleeves so that you could see parts of her bra straps and the hair in her armpits. She wore her hair cut straight across her eyebrows and hanging straight down. In summer her skin freckled. I loved her; and that love made me more than ordinarily receptive the day she turned to me in our Grade Eleven English class and said, "I've got *Parasites of Heaven*. I've just read it. It's great. You wanna read it?"

I did. *Parasites of Heaven* was Leonard Cohen's newest book, which at that time and place meant that every phrase in it would be suffused with glamour, and not only that, but after I had read a couple of pages, Alistair would grab the book from me, and then Ned would grab it from him.

Where did the glamour come from? Well, Alistair and Ned had both come from Pinky, Saskatchewan, where they had spent most of their growing-up running through fields and then standing in silence in the middle of roads waiting for a car to come along or for something else to happen. I had come from Hinton, and then (after a year and a half in North Van), from Allenby Landing, a small pulp mill town a hundred miles up the coast. Pamela had come from a little place outside White-

41

horse and it seemed had spent her growing-up years either in the bush or in a little woodshed talking to a chipmunk named Earlybird. Then, all together, it seemed, we had arrived at the British Properties in West Vancouver, the richest section of the richest suburb in Canada, where I remember five or six of us in bathing suits sitting around a steamy indoor swimming pool in a private home, reciting poems about elves derived from e.e. cummings and Gerard Manley Hopkins. We were in the right place at the right time, and almost overnight we turned from rural kids smelling of the bush into what Vancouverites knew as "West Vancouver kids," hippies, arrogant and beautiful in our pea jackets and duffle coats — the perfect illustration of what was known then as the "generation gap." Everywhere you turned another magazine article took it up. What the hippies most wanted, the articles said, was to shame their rigid elders into accepting a new outlook on life.

We read these articles greedily, and for two reasons. First, they contained images of what we wanted to look like. This was essential: if the magazines hadn't contained photographs of Bob Dylan and Marianne Faithful, say, we wouldn't have brought such a sustained interest to the stories they were cranking out. The pictures fascinated us, they provided lessons in style, and for this reason they were a lot more important — a lot more open to study, you might say — than the text that accompanied them.

But the text (and this was the other reason we read these articles so greedily), the text offered us exactly what we wanted to read, as if all those apparently judicious sentences were really no more than buds of words secreted by the pictures that accompanied them. And without exception, these word-buds bloomed into a wonderful idea: if you were under 25, you were beautiful enough, virtuous enough, to provide lessons in ethics to the larger world.

Marvelous! But also inadequate. And really, beside the point. Because by stressing the ethical side of things, this argument entirely overlooked the activity of play-acting we were engaged in, an activity so intoxicating that many of us awoke years later with a kind of psychological hangover and only the fuzziest notion of what had occurred.

Think again of those photographs that were constantly appearing in the magazines, those pictures of Dylan, Faithful, Donovan, Joni Mitchell, Jimi Hendrix and so on and so forth. What did they offer if not a kind of image bank of style? There they were: all you had to do was pick through them, looking for details of hair and dress it would be possible to incorporate into your own persona. And what seriousness, what excitement went into this activity! If *Newsweek* had a cover story on Dylan and the "folk-rockers", say, you would quickly leaf through the magazine and then freeze when you got to the pages in which the story appeared, as still as a statue, your cigarette held out, intent, *fascinated.*

And it wasn't just the styles of heroes. Things themselves — certain kinds of jeans, Navy pea coats, Huck Finn caps, World War Two greatcoats made of itchy wool, off-road motorcycles, leather vests, moccasins — things themselves were swallowed up the way we would later swallow glasses of draft in Vancouver's beer parlours, and with much the same result. That is, you remained aware of the reality of the situation around you but only in the way a drunken man might, a fact that was noticeable not just at the gatherings in which hippies got together to look at each other, but also in the department stores in which the things were bought — for us, in particular, the paradise for bourgeois teenagers that Eaton's Park Royal started operating around this time.

These were the years from 1965 to 1970. I began them in West Vancouver and ended them driving back up to Canada from Houston, Texas; and when I think of them now I remember the explosive romanticism of the time and the extraordinary difficulty I had in finding a place in the world. I would get into the most horrible fights at home, and even went through a period where for some months I refused to talk to my parents: essentially I resembled my peers in that I lived in a world of my own creation and ignored the larger world except when it fed that creation. Something extraordinarily new hung in the air, and while you went through a lot of pain trying to get close to that newness, it felt worth it. It seemed that nothing like it had ever appeared before.

2

It had, though, even if not in the same form. The growth of the hippie movement coincided with a social crisis. And I think that our intoxication in rich West Vancouver stemmed from the fact that we were allowed to make theatre out of this crisis, to turn the realities of the sixties into a setting for self-display. This achievement — as well as the margin of safety which made it possible — had occurred before. In the last section of *In Search of Lost Time*, Marcel Proust describes the effect of the First World War on the young women of his milieu:

> As if by the germination of a tiny quantity of yeast, apparently of spontaneous generation, young women ... now wore Egyptian tunics, straight and dark and very "war," over very short skirts; they wore shoes with ankle-straps recalling the buskin as worn by Talma, or else long gaiters recalling those of our dear boys at the front. ... the fashion now was for rings or bracelets made out of fragments of exploded shells or copper bands from 75-millimeter ammunition, and for cigarette lighters constructed out of two English pennies to which a soldier, in his dugout, had succeeded in giving a patina so beautiful that the profile of Queen Victoria looked as if it had been drawn by the hand of Pisanello.

Proust goes on to make an ethical argument about all this (the exact opposite of the one that was made about us hippies, by the way). But for the moment let me put that argument aside and concentrate instead on the beauty of the "patina" that Proust describes.

In what did this beauty lie? To start with, it lay in the simple physical appeal of the English pennies. But more deeply, the pennies' patina of use made visible the glamour that emanates from things that seem to hold in a concentrated form the experiences denied their beholder. You can see Proust's women: young and frivolous, with nothing to do, they had been caught up first in a fever of pacifism; then, when the chips were down, patriotism had taken over, and now they wandered the stores of Paris with their heads full of images of war, looking for something that would represent the crisis they were living through, something both stylish and evocative.

And what could fit the bill better than a lighter made out of two English pennies? Such an object wasn't just small and pretty; it was emblematic, since these pennies which had been handled by a soldier in the trenches had the aura of wartime experience around them in an especially intimate way — an aura that not incidentally included death, since it was often through a soldier's death that the pennies found their way into the stores.

Fifty years later a similar aura bewitched us students. There were the *new* clothes — the miniskirts, suede coats and shirts with puffy sleeves. But there were also the *old* clothes — the granny dresses, sport coats, logging boots and Army jackets — that spoke of adult experience, the realities of war and work and a life that contained history. Lacking experience of our own, caught up in a crisis from which we were buffered by money and class (the phenomenon that produced Leonard Cohen's popularity was almost entirely an upper-middle-class phenomenon) but which we wanted to somehow be part of, to master and, so to speak, represent in ourselves, we "put on" experience in the form of clothes that helped us feel adequate to the situation we were living through. In fact, appropriating the experience of others by wearing their dress was central to the dream-life of the sixties as far as we students were concerned. Packed away in high-toned suburbias where there was nothing to do, where the bustle of work was nonexistent and where many of us couldn't open the newspaper until our dads had finished with it, we succumbed to the glamour of other people's experience the way children do to the glamour of aggressive, emotionally charged words when they are first learning to read. We were like

Proust's haute monde, subtly starved; hence the fierce attention we brought to the clothes smelling like old chesterfields in the St. Vincent de Paul down on East Hastings, to the black and white photographs on the inside covers of *Blonde on Blonde*, and to songs like "Cowgirl in the Sand" and "Hey Joe," in which we found a world where words like "road," "death" and "night" once more had meaning.

By around the age of twelve taste had come into play. Style had become a personal matter; and that entire self-conscious, subtle and yet utterly serious appropriation of the glamour of other people and their things that started with the movies had reached an apotheosis. You watched Jimi Hendrix; you mimicked his dress, his moves. Sometimes you imitated them directly; more often, you adopted a watered-down version of their extreme presence. The trick was to incorporate their aura of beauty and power, the things every adolescent most wants, into your own much-pondered persona, to simultaneously neutralize the actuality of the experience these living objects expressed and retain the glamour of that experience in the form of fashion. It was a poignant — and, as Cohen recognized – a powerful trick, the trick at the very heart of consumer culture.

3

Cohen's poems 'The Music Crept By Us', 'What I'm Doing Here' (from *Flowers for Hitler*), 'The Genius' and 'Angels' (from *The Spice-Box of Earth*) show this trick at work. The heroic pose, the lyrics using the language of love to evoke grotesque subject matter, the narcissism, the coy glamorization of failure and terror — all this hit home to me and my teenage friends. Of course we didn't have any real understanding of the severity and pain of failure. But in Cohen's poems, just as in songs like "Desolation Row," we found a romantic mode of writing that provided an access to a realm of experience that might otherwise have proved overpowering and beyond our ability to assimilate.

And how much beauty Cohen had at his command! For all my subsequent disenchantment, much of his early poetry fell upon me like leaves from a tree in a fairy tale. Failure and grief were elements in the work, for sure. But from the start Cohen's boulevardier gallantry and Prevert-like lyricism — that whole leafy bower of fine writing — ensured that my daydreaming adolescent mind could enter his world without fear and rock back and forth in time to the sweetest of tunes.

The fact is, I loved Cohen's poems. His combination of stylized metropolitan reality with the most old-fashioned and incantatory elements of the ballad tradition allowed him to produce poetry so intoxicating to me that his very books seemed enchanted. Poetic content and the actual physical reality of the pages could hardly be separated; and when I moved to Texas and came across an American edition of Cohen's work in which the verses were squeezed together in a standardized format, I experienced an abrupt disillusionment: it was as if the spirit concentrated in the original typography had been somehow dissipated.

So why did I stop reading him? Well, as with e.e. cummings, another poet I admired, the very intoxication I felt marks the point at which Cohen's weaknesses can be observed: the playing to an audience, the easy stylization of experience. *Vanity* was Cohen's element, just as a black leather sportscoat was his favoured dress, and the consequent staging of the personality that I now sense everywhere in his work meant that an infatuated intelligence instead of an alert one was the order of the day so far as his readers were concerned.

The demand for an infatuated surrender to the image implicit in his work can be sensed everywhere in Cohen's verses. Consider the following lines from "You Have the Lovers" (a poem that transfixed me when I was seventeen):

> You stand beside the bed weeping with happiness,
> you carefully peel away the sheets
> from the slow-moving bodies.
> Your eyes are filled with tears, you barely make out
> 　the lovers.
> As you undress you sing out, and your voice is
> 　magnificent

because now you believe it is the first human voice
heard in that room.
The garments you let fall grow into vines.
You climb into bed and recover the flesh.

This swaying, incantatory verse communicates a dream
experience. Instead of a line whose precision shows you the real
world, Cohen offers a line whose images of slow-moving bodies,
of singing and tears, are suffused with a surrender to distance,
and so loosely attached to the world that only someone in love
with an image rather than a reality could make use of it.

The truth is, experiencing Cohen was uncannily like experiencing infatuated love. And it was the same with Bob Dylan and
the rest of the sixties crew. When my friends and I listened to
records, sitting in living rooms facing each other, our empa-
thetic distraction was so striking that we seemed to be under a
spell, our personalities not so much muted as obliterated. Sitting
impassive before each other, we moved as slowly and carefully as
woodsmen around a fire. In fact, inspired by the music, we were
ourselves on display, each of us an inhabitant of Highway 61,
and you would have had to have seen this in us to know just how
intimately linked we were to the women described by Proust.

Sad to say, we suffered from the same ludicrous, paralyzing fascination with the image (Marianne Faithful's hair, Bob Dylan's
cheeks) that made the *haut monde* such a great subject in Proust's
book. Not only did a person's clothes speak far more decisively to
us than anything that came out of his mouth; language itself was
degraded to a mere aspect of appearance. Slowly you'd push your
hair back behind your ears, take a toke, and to some comment
say, "Far out man." In the same way that sunglasses mask the
eyes' complexity, producing an image at once blank and impassive, we students attempted to mask every trace of the intimate, perplexed, thoughtful aspects of the voice. Even your laugh
became something you attempted to make wise and strong: too
bad for you if the fresh notes of adolescence poured forth.

This effort at dissimulation was of course rooted in adolescent
uncertainty. But we were also addicted to images. And while

much was made in those days of the need for "openness," our breathtakingly formulaic approach to language was far less the result of "openness" than it was a symptom of the inner rigidity of those who, in surrendering themselves to appearance, can no longer trust themselves to speak.

4

So was it all bad? Not entirely.

We had spent our childhoods in the bush. Neither I nor my friends had seen a TV set until we were ten or eleven. And then, with the suddenness of a riptide, everything changed. The surrender to the image which characterized our reading of Cohen, the fascinated way we listened to "Desolation Row" and which so worried our parents — these responses showed our reaction to the change; they revealed our stunned, almost sleepwalking embrace of the new environment we had come to.

At least that was what our parents saw. But from another point of view this distracted surrender enabled us to find a space for reverie. We had known reverie in the bush. We had daydreamed for hours. But now we were in a world that didn't encourage daydreaming at all. Once you understand this, you can begin to understand the embryonic morality that the poets and singers who fascinated us were trying to give birth to.

Think of the fairy-tale figures in Neil Young's "Sugar Mountain," the images of slow-moving bodies in Cohen's "You Have the Lovers," the dreamlike landscapes in Bob Dylan's "Visions of Johanna" and Phil Ochs's "Pleasures of the Harbour." In all these works, incantation took precedence. Instead of an abrupt line, the line of a rapper, say, full of shocks that ask to be met by an aggressive presence of mind, these poets gave the reader or listener a line imbued with a sense of distance. Their works relaxed him, thereby making him receptive to the ceremonial presence of the image. The boundaries between dream and reality were worn away by the sway of the words.

And so these works were therapeutic, aids to fantasy in an environment which stressed in a hundred different ways that nothing was less useful than the ability to daydream, nothing more important than the concentrated, disciplined intelligence. It was paradise, all right, the British Properties in the mid-sixties. But, oh, those endless sidewalks! Those chores! That self-conscious punctuality and keep-your-nose-to-the-grindstone work ethic! Those cocktail parties and screaming fights!

Think of it like this, and the retreat into the world of the dream which characterized me and my friends can be better understood. Remember Mister Natural? The idea of going into the country — to a cabin, with tall grasses growing outside the door, with boredom, silence and wind part of your life, with your old lady baking bread while you played the flute and got your shit together — buried in this idea was a relationship to the world my friends and I had known as kids. Certainly our arguments were confused; parts were ludicrous. Still, we saw something: we saw that for those who have assimilated the disciplines of contemporary life, the image which intoxicates isn't the one that induces a daydreaming surrender. No, the image which intoxicates is the one that provides the maximum stimulus for the alert consciousness — in the realm of feeling, the image which provokes those "brief and bestial emotions" that Valery mentions in an essay he wrote on city life and which in our own time has led to pop culture of an almost pornographic crudeness. This is the "stigmata that life in a metropolis inflicts upon love," and I believe that the best way to understand the romanticism of the sixties is to see it as a quickly swept-away reaction to that stigmata. I don't bother with Cohen now, but when I was writing love poems to my first real girlfriend, his imagery made its way unerringly into my lines.

Stan Persky's Enormous Reasonableness

1

S tan Persky lives in Kitsilano, a predominantly white section of Vancouver across the Burrard Bridge from downtown. More precisely, he lives on York Street near Cornwall Avenue, an area close to the beach where women in their thirties wear Spandex biking shorts and young men with heavily muscled arms spike basketballs and shout at each other like American blacks. Renovated houses, high cedar fences, bright stone walls and immaculate sidewalks all make it a pleasure to walk there in the morning sun.

So my first sight of Persky's house came as a shock. An old convertible — a junker — sat out in front. The steps — the house was set on a small hill — were worn, and the house was a brown hulk, pushed at on the side by an enormous, half-wild hedge. I felt disillusionment: the address, as well as Persky's notoriety, had led me to expect something grander. But as I stepped onto the porch everything snapped into place. The chipped concrete steps, the shabby lawn, the hedge, the old door with its glass oval and manual buzzer that you turned with thumb and finger: it was a hippie house, no different from the ones I'd known almost twenty years ago. On the porch I even thought I smelled cat piss.

Then another shock: Persky himself. Sloppy jeans (cut graph-

ically full: I thought, "Dogpatch jeans"), an old black T-shirt,
big bum, big gut; and long strands of hair combed old-man style
across a balding head animated by bright eyes. I had met him
before, but standing now in his doorway, he was like the resi-
dent witch, his body and clothes as outrageous in their way as a
long whiskered chin and black dress. Then all at once the seedi-
ness disappeared, erased by a soft, curving, intensely welcoming
smile. (People can change: fifteen years later, Persky had become
a pleasant-looking man in his sixties, especially appealing in his
black European sports cap.)

"Serafin. Come on in," he said, and I felt immediately at ease.

Inside the house that sense of the old hippie world was even
stronger. It was there in the shadowy halls, the big communal
kitchen, the drawn floor-to-ceiling curtains, the shabby book-
cases and old furniture — even in the piles of paper that were
everywhere. It was a place (protected and darkened by the hedge,
darkened by the curtains) that was both eccentric and secure. It
had a charm, the charm of shyness, shabbiness, casualness, and
once past the shyness, a remarkable willingness to be open to
inspection.

Describing Persky to me, his friend Brian Fawcett had used
a metaphor. "He's Caliban. Years ago we put on *The Tempest*
and Stan played Caliban. That's his persona. And it's the true
Caliban. He insists that intelligence that doesn't have the gross-
ness of the body is nothing. Look at him and his place and it's like
he's made a deliberate, quite careful decision not to be involved
in matters of taste at any level of his life." And as I watched Persky make coffee and answer the phone, which seemed to ring
constantly ("Yeah, yeah, he's just raging nuts," he said at one
point, forgetting the interview, caught up in the gossip that was
being related to him), as I watched the awkward movements his
body forced on him, and noticed his combination of shyness and
exuberance, his willingness to say exactly what was on his mind,
I did see, if not the darkness of Caliban — for Persky is sweet-
tempered — at least something of Caliban's earthiness. Here in
his own place Persky seemed at home with himself, a man who
had worked hard to make himself what he was.

2

He was born in Chicago and moved to San Francisco when he was a teenager; there he became friends with Allen Ginsberg and Peter Orlovsky. While still in his teens he joined the US Navy, which allowed him to travel to Naples and Paris, then, when that was over, he came back to Frisco and in the mid-sixties emigrated to Vancouver to study at the University of British Columbia (where as a student activist he climbed up on tables in the cafeteria and, "shaking with nervousness," as he says, "shouted politely" at people to get their attention). He wrote poetry, and quickly became one of the central figures in the literary scene that was emerging in the city; in particular he gained a name as an editor and publisher, someone who was involved with most of the magazines of the time (and still is: from *Tish*, *The Georgia Straight* and *The Western Voice*, among others, he has gone on to *Books in Canada* and the web magazine *Dooney's Café*.)

In the late seventies, he stopped writing poetry and, sensing an audience, began producing book after book of left-wing political journalism, starting with *Son of Socred* and continuing through *At the Lenin Shipyard*, *Bennett II*, and *America, the Last Domino*. He got a job teaching philosophy and political science at Capilano College, where he still works, began appearing on BCTV as a sort of left-wing commentator on local news, and in general became something of a Socratic figure in the jumpy and sometimes vicious world of BC politics. His good temper and common sense made him admired; the persona in his writing — if you didn't know him — would make you think of a big reasonable fellow who wore a beard and perhaps wrote with his sleeves rolled up. And throughout all this, in the Navy, in Paris and Naples, in San Francisco, then in Vancouver, he was taking young men to bed and being taken by them, falling desperately in love and, as he said of a five-year affair in Vancouver, becoming "agonized over it all." None of that showed up in his writing until this year. Then out of nowhere, as it were, *Buddy's* appeared — a revelatory book, and to me the best thing Persky

had written — and now here we were in his kitchen discussing
whether or not there was such a thing as a homosexual.

It was an argument we had had earlier, at the book launch for
Buddy's. (For me a difficult occasion: I had been as nervous as
Persky was exuberant, and when we finally got a few moments to
talk to each other, I had blurted out the first thing that came to
mind, something about what it was like to move from writing as
a political figure to writing as a homosexual. Persky said something to the effect that there was no such thing as a homosexual.
I had disagreed; we argued a bit; then we promised each other
we would come back to it later.) Now we did, and Persky was
prepared. He had made some notes, and as he spoke he referred
to the notes. He said that he wanted to talk about the "political
contradictions" that his book involved.

But he started with our earlier argument, and at first he was
careful, even a little nervous, speaking so deliberately that I could
see the teacher in him. "In *Buddy's*," he said, "I found myself
using words like 'homoerotic' and 'ephebe' — in part so as not to
be accused of molesting young boys! I used these words because
they aren't politically loaded, they don't have a premeaning that
determines their usage. I resist the use of the term "homosexual"
as an identifier except as a political term, i.e., if there's someone
out there who doesn't like homosexuals, I'm willing to be one.
The word is loaded, as *left-handed, philosopher, college instructor*
aren't. The other part of the resistance is that it just isn't true.
For example, last night I was a magazine mailer and *New Directions* collective member. I wasn't a homosexual. In the magazine
I was an author of a judicial commentary. Earlier in the day I was
a union member at Capilano College. It goes on and on."

3

All this was clear; but it was a bit like a political line, and I must
have seemed skeptical. Because as Persky kept talking he gradually changed tack and began to speak more loosely and openly.
Finally he said, "Like everyone else, I have mixed feelings about
homosexuality. Personally, I like its forbiddenness. It connects

with my resistance to conventionality, bourgeois society, etc. I like the outlaw side of it. Of course I defend bourgeois homosexual couples watering plants, etc., but I'm not interested in that. I don't especially understand that, any more than you might understand my interest in ephebes." He glanced at me, giving me a chance to say something, and when I didn't he kept on talking, still struggling with his earlier thought about "political contradictions." Then he said something that impressed me. "The ones that I desire are indeed the ones that I desire. Politically, this leads to great contradictions. But I didn't create those contradictions. I didn't create the fact that those I desire stand on street corners soliciting. But my concerns about that remain."

The ones that I desire are indeed the ones that I desire. There was a challenge, even a rebuke in that. The statement pointed to Persky's refusal to deviate from what he was, his refusal to capitulate to what others might think his practice ought to be. That refusal was in *Buddy's*, and while it was true, as Persky insisted, that the book was indebted to Roland Barthes, what was essential about the book wasn't the writing that brought Barthes to mind — the occasional preciosities, and dainty movement from anecdote to analysis — but the graphic portrayal of a sexual life. The great thing about the book, I had felt when I read it, was its sheer joy in telling stories in all their detail — and as I talked to Persky I noticed this joy. His conversation was quick, digressive, constantly spilling from one thing to another. When I asked him about that, mentioning the happiness in the book, and adding that in my experience there was a lot of wistfulness in gay literature, he responded quickly.

"No, I don't feel that. Because Barthes is my guide in *Buddy's* I'm determinedly seeing all these things as pleasures. Though towards the end of the book I'm getting a little weary of all this!" And here he exploded with laughter. "Seeing these guys not as Eros, Cupid, etc., which is what I call them in the book, but as young guys with fucked-up lives. Take Bret" — one of the characters in *Buddy's*. "He's a beautiful young man and all that in my story, but he had had a disastrous life in the past year, including an attempted suicide."

Persky paused. "I seem to be writing this without regrets. I am not looking for the kind of romantic love that you might be looking for. It's true that earlier on I was much more agonized about love, but now the world of desire seems fairly comic to me. I love the stories. In the gay world love stories are a basic mode of exchange. Cupid's basic mode of exchange is gossip. He hated that when I pointed it out to him!

"There's a biographical point here. I grew up in the same homophobic America as everybody else. And at the age of 14 or 15 I was terrified by it all, as well as being additionally terrified by any contact with human beings. I was terrified at the junior prom. But early on, from about 16, I was in contact with Allen Ginsberg, then later on from about 18 I was in contact with Jack Spicer and Robert Duncan, so I was in a society where homosexuality was taken for granted. Then the Navy. And the Navy was nice enough to ship me to Naples, and gave me time to go to Paris where Ginsberg and Orlovsky were staying at 9, rue Git-le-coeur, the Beat Hotel. So I was in unusually safe surroundings. Talk about insults! I couldn't get *wounded* by the foreign language. And I remember very distinctly, at about 19 or 20, sucking off this guy's cock and thinking, I really like this. This was a phenomenological fact for me. Boy, that was about the clearest moment I've had on this very complicated subject. In the Navy there wasn't a moment that I wasn't in love, and I remember being very terrified about this. But those French boys — Luc and Jackie — weren't disturbed about it at all."

And Canada?

"Oh, I loved Canada. I was immediately at home here. And I loved the boys. They were different, reticent; and they were sexually unafraid, willing to try different things. I was in love from the first minute I was in Canada."

Hearing this about Canada, I was reminded of something else that had struck me in *Buddy's* — and that was my sense of seeing Vancouver in a way I never had before. Its bars and apartment buildings, its street corners and back doors and storefronts — the entire West End in fact — were made alluringly distinct, as if flooded with a Mediterranean light, by the sexual desire animating the gaze looking at them. This warm clear world was very different from the world of left-wing BC politics that Persky was usually associated with. That was a world of rain and umbrellas, big men and women, hoarse voices trying to make a point in stuffy halls. That other world was where Persky was best known, and when I asked him about it he responded with a sort of critical tenderness that made his statements gentler than they appear on the page.

He said, "I'm in favour of social justice, so that puts me on the left. I'm engaged with the left and I regard that as more important than undoing any of the mistakes that the left might make.

"At the same time I'm appalled by the left" — and this word, "appalled," was one he would use again and again. "Just appalled. I have a sense of humour. I remember one time at a radical left meeting in the seventies — an awful meeting, horrible — I just sort of shyly got up and wrote on the blackboard, 'MAO HAS A BIG DONG.' Well, this was silly and people hated me for it, but I was just oppressed by the righteousness and heaviness of what was going on."

I mentioned writing.

"There's no excuse for bad prose, and there's especially no excuse for bad left prose. I'm always appalled by the writing. What I tell people is, 'You guys ought to lift your eyes high enough above the barricades to notice that Langara College has a journalism school in this town. You ought to forget your leftist views for a moment and learn how to write a lead.' I compare their stuff to the Vancouver *Province*. They're appalled when I throw the *Province* at them as a model. But I do a lot of that. I'm self-confident enough now that I'm not intimidated. I say, 'You people are contemptuous of your readers. I find you insufferably arrogant in not writing warmly and clearly enough to attract readers.'"

We talked about Randy Shilts's book *And the Band Played On*. The book had impressed Persky, and he had used it in an article he had written for *This Magazine* on some of the issues surrounding AIDS. This article — essentially a report on how an unlikely coalition of the left and right in BC had ended up producing an intelligent piece of legislation outlining what should be done if someone "willfully or carelessly" spread AIDS to others — was clear and judicious, animated by reason. Persky had worked hard for this reasonableness, and it had got him in trouble.

"Gay leftists hate Shilts's book," he said. "They think he's internalized self-hatred. They blame Shilts for the emphasis on Patient Zero — Gaetan Dugas. They feel that Shilts was on the side of those people who wanted the bathhouses closed. Well, I cited some of what he reported on, and said that interestingly enough these are the very issues that are being debated in BC. The response to that from the gay left was vitriolic, particularly in *Rites Magazine*, which is a Toronto mag. They just conflated Shilts and me. There's a piece in there by George Smith, who's a blustery sociologist, which is really a hack job, the worst kind of denunciatory propaganda. This attacking people on your own side — like the attack on Shilts, who really just produced a superb piece of reportage — I've always been clear that I think this is the most destructive thing the left can engage in. It's understandable if you're part of the viewpoint that's marginalized — as leftists are in this society — you can get paranoid, etc. But you have to get past that. I try to. I've got a large populist streak in me; I want to communicate. I'm also very practical-minded, so I'm willing to work for what can be done."

4

I had begun to see what this meant. Sitting across from me in his worn-out T-shirt, smoking, digressing, trying out one idea after another — "I have opinions on everything," he said with a laugh — what kept coming across was the idea of "service."

Politics was service; writing was service. He would see something that he could do, and he would try to do it. He was constantly at work, and the evidence was there in the piles of paper that filled his house. Brian Fawcett had said to me that Persky was an educator, a teacher, someone who encouraged at any cost free public discourse; "... there's this enormous reasonableness, this complete willingness to consider another side. There's no bitterness in him, just a huge courage."

Fawcett spoke sharply about Persky's relationship to the left. He felt that while Persky had remained true to himself and his principles of reasonableness and open discourse, the left had moved, slipping down into fundamentalism and a kind of denial of reality.

Persky was kinder than that — in all that he said it was plain that the left was his community. But listening to him I could understand what Fawcett meant. There was a subtlety in his position: on the one hand he was someone who could operate only as he was (he spoke for instance of how bored he got at NDP meetings "because so much of reality is cut off; desire, for instance,"); on the other hand he had a deep respect for the actuality of the situation that confronted him. He mentioned his admiration for people like Ginsberg, and spoke of how he himself tried to be as "effusive as necessary in public, so the public doesn't fall asleep." "If the *Province* gave me 500 words a day," he said, "I would try to write to fit the format of the paper and still get across some of the things I want to say. And if I'm on TV and they ask for 30 seconds, I'll give them 30 seconds. I think it's a good idea to have some respect for the situation you're in."

This side of Persky — the realistic, adaptable side — was foreign to much of the left that I knew, and when I mentioned this to Persky he looked worried. Yet he kept returning to the same themes: being responsible, using reason. He was worried that what he called "the idea of legitimate authority" had all but disappeared. He mentioned the situation he had described earlier, when legislation was passed in BC to deal with the "willful" spreading of AIDS.

Persky said, "Even after the legislation was passed and it was plain that nobody was being hauled off the streets or anything like that, people were recalling grandmothers incarcerated in the Second World War. It was overblown. It did nobody any good. And that's the problem — reactions like that that pay no attention to the actual nature of what is being legislated. We have no sense of what it's like to have someone who's a public guardian. Our sense of legitimate authority has just dwindled. We have no feeling for what it would be like — authority that doesn't chafe.

"Then again, sometimes you see people — I think David Suzuki is one of them — that have a real authority. When somebody is on — when they've got their hands on something and they're moving with it — they operate with a kind of non-egotistical energy that's very attractive and draws people to them. Suzuki, I think, has acquired that by knowing his own mind, by not deceiving people. And you can find it in yourself. You go to a meeting, for instance, and for one reason or another you're called on to lead it. Usually you do so-so. But at other times, at rare moments, you have this sense of conviction and certitude. You can see yourself being useful, and others are grateful to you for it. That's how I'd like to be."

About a month later I stood with Persky on his porch. He was wearing another T-shirt that was just as worn out as the first one. We looked at the new concrete curb — so smooth and white — that had been put in around his house since I had last been there. It looked completely out of place, and when I remarked on this, Persky said, "Dust. It was dust that brought that curb. It was still a little countryish around here, a little dusty. Well, I liked that. But the neighbours have nice cars and they didn't want dust on their cars. So there you are."

Sailors

1

On this sunny day at CenTerm — Vancouver's Centennial Terminal, at the foot of Hastings — the bright orange dock cranes, the bright red Canadian Fishing Company warehouse with its white silos in front of it (the silos making the warehouse look like a grain elevator), the stacks of brightly coloured Hyundai cargo containers and the gleaming tractor-trailers that fill the parking lot all seem like a stage set for the small, elegant, blue-painted Mission for Seafarers house, on whose wide porch this afternoon male and female Russian sailors are drinking coffee and smoking cigarettes.

Inside, sitting in a row of old telephone booths under old round clocks that showed the time in a number of cities, including London and Vancouver, other Russian men and women are using phone cards to call home. "The cards cost five dollars," Josephine Enriquez, the Filipino-born receptionist, says. "They can have local calls for free."

One man waiting to make a call has gold fillings all along his upper teeth, a black beard, a Russian face with narrow cat's eyes and Slavic cheekbones. He grins at me. He's been watching Josephine and me talk; now he wants to tell me how poor they are, he and his fellow seafarers. Using hand gestures, he explains how four or five people will use one phone card. "Just talk, wife."

He makes a gesture, indicating the next person. "Talk, husband."
Signalling quick, quick. "Talk, wife."

He laughs and leans forward to touch my shoulder. I can smell
beer on his breath. "No money." He smiles, shows me the money
in the pocket of his black jeans. A loonie, a dime, some pennies.

Another man comes into the small office to talk to him, a
shorter man wearing freshly laundered blue jeans and a white T-
shirt tucked into the jeans. Clean-shaven, with large alert eyes,
this younger man looks steadily at his tough-looking companion.
Soon they're arguing in Russian. The older sailor, talking loudly,
demonstratively shows the younger man the same loonie, dime
and pennies that he showed me. It's clear he was supposed to
help pay for something. The younger man looks at him quietly
for a moment, then walks away into the big, comfortable common room.

Their ship is a fishing boat, Josephine says. She tells me about
another Russian fishing boat that docked last year in North Vancouver. The owner left the ship. "The seamen didn't have any
money: no salary. They were deported back to Russia. You see,
they didn't have visas."

The sailor with the gold teeth listens to us, smiling. He wants
to tell us something but doesn't have the words for it, so he talks
quickly in Russian. Trying to get me to understand him he hugs
me, then hugs me again.

Glancing at the man to include him in the conversation, I ask
Josephine about the female Russians. Are they wives?

"No. They are crew. They do cleaning, housekeeping. For the
fishing boat."

I ask her how many are in the crew. She doesn't know. "Maybe
fifty?"

This the sailor understands. He says, "No. Hundred twenty-
five. Two crew." Using hand gestures again, he sketches two
shifts. One sleeping: he puts his head sideways on his hands.
One working: he moves his body up.

He hugs me again; he doesn't want to go. He's happy to be talking to someone besides the usual gang. And I think, looking into

the common room where on this beautiful afternoon other Russians are watching a music video on TV and flipping through old copies of Time magazine: Why are they hanging around?

2

Things have changed. The Reverend William Pike, the senior port chaplain, tells me that the Mission for Seafarers — a mildly religious organization funded by individual donations, contributions from the port of Vancouver and fund-raising events — services "about 3,000 ships per year, including the ones at Roberts Bank, which we also serve. The Mission deals with about 26,000 sailors a year. Roughly 20 to 25 sailors a day."

"You rarely see sailors downtown," I say.

"No," Josephine says. "There's the Japanese students — the ones going to shipping school. They come in on the something Maru. What is it called? I can't remember. They wear uniforms. You see them downtown. That's the only ones left that wear uniforms. There's no military sailors. So the seamen don't stand out."

"That's right," Reverend Pike says. "The sailors aren't visible any more. Given the cosmopolitan, international nature of Vancouver they just fit in. They just disappear into the crowd. And of course they don't wear uniforms. The old merchant navy used to, but nobody does any more."

And the clothes the sailors wear — like the clothes in the thrift shop the Mission runs, each item selling for a dollar — these are the standard clothes seen everywhere in the world now: jeans, T-shirts, sweaters, windbreakers, running shoes.

"There used to be regular dances, two or three times a week. Entertainment was provided. Hostesses came in. They were under strict supervision of course and the sailors couldn't leave with them. Back then the sailors had time. Now they're in and out, sometimes in less than a day. Their time off is very limited. That's made a great difference." The Reverend pauses for a moment. "And there's something else too. The nationalities of the seafarers have changed. There used to be Scandinavian, European sailors. Now, with the global economy, the owners of the ships hire the cheapest labourers, the seafarers they can pay least to. And that usually means Asian and Filipino."

Reverend Pike tells me about an international three-tiered scale of wages, the highest for North Americans, the next highest for Europeans, the lowest for Asians. "Which means of course that they hire Asian crewmen. So instead of having many Norwegians, Polish, etc., you have Filipinos, Indians, Chinese. We offer amenities geared to this. We can't offer the same kind of entertainment that we used to, dances etc. Cultural differences come into play."

"They can check their e-mail," Josephine says. "Use the phones. Attend mass. We have a pool table, ping-pong. A clothing store and general store. We have coffee. And a place to sit and relax. But if they want to go to a mall, we show them how to get to Pacific Centre. And usually they want to go to a restaurant."

What restaurants, though?

"Greeks — maybe they will go to a Greek restaurant. Maybe on West Broadway, you know. Or on Davie. Stephos is there. Or they will go to Calypso. And on Commercial Drive. The Chinese go to Chinatown. The Russians, I don't know. There is a Russian restaurant on Broadway and Cambie. But I think it is very expensive."

I ask what they might shop for.

"Shoes, clothes, electronics. But they find that things are expensive. It's better in the States, especially in Portland. They will go to restaurants, do some sight-seeing. If they have friends they will see them. If they have friends they won't come here!" She laughs, then tells me that a French cable ship was coming in. "Lots of Filipinos on that ship. They come when the cruise ships are over. They will dock there and stay for a whole six months. The seamen live on board the ship. They have a nice ship."

Conrado Ambido — a Filipino like Josephine, a relaxed, articulate man who has been at the Mission thirty years and who works now as a driver, picking up the sailors — Conrado tells me they might go to girlie shows at the Drake or the No. 5 Orange.

"Mind you, they can buy beer here. They have to drink it here. They can't drink up to their eyeballs. Two, maybe three beers."

I ask about money.

"They don't earn much. The Russians — if you convert the Russian rubles — they make maybe $300, $400 a month. That won't go very far in Vancouver."

I think: But it might go far in Russia.

"So the sailors —"

Conrado gently corrects me. "No. Seamen. Sailors are more like uniformed people. You hardly ever have them. They're seamen. They don't wear uniforms. It's all civilian dress now."

"Why do the Russians hang around the Mission?"

"Because they are strangers. They don't know where to go. If they were a Greek crew, they might go up to West Broadway, where the restaurants are. The Chinese go to Chinatown. Same with Koreans, they learn where the Korean hangouts are. The Filipino, they speak pretty well English. They can find their way around. The difficulty comes with the Russians. They can hardly speak English. I would imagine they would have difficulty taking, say, a bus."

"What do the seamen think about Vancouver?"

He makes a little shrug. "Filipinos find it expensive. Cigarettes. Seventy dollars a carton!"

3

Before coming to the Mission, crossing over the land bridge at the bottom of Main, I had talked briefly with a woman drinking from a huge can of beer. She said, "This is a bum area." I agreed; then I said that I found it evocative: a quarter century earlier I had lived nearby. "Oh well, for you it's a trip down memory lane. Not for me. I suppose you could find it aesthetically pleasing though."

She was right; I did. The extraordinary economic dynamism which was evident at CenTerm had transformed the city. Now it was transforming the area around the docks; and with its mixture of ocean light, seagulls, bright cranes, container cargos, railroad

tracks, brick buildings that were being renovated and new buildings that catered to the young, it seemed to me the most interesting, maybe even the most beautiful part of Vancouver.

I wasn't alone in this judgement. Walking towards the Mission,
I passed a young man with a bright light and a metal reflector
photographing a young woman in a dress like a tutu, folds and
folds of white chiffon going to mid-thigh; she wore black, high-
topped shoes. A little further along I passed another group taking photos, young people dressed in dark clothes and narrow
fashionable glasses. (But then — almost as if to keep my judge-
ments in check — a woman ran past me, a drug addict with stick
legs, stick arms, wearing floppy shorts and a floppy T-shirt, running with her arms jerking oddly, the entire skull of her face visible so that she looked like an Auschwitz survivor.)

The area was changing. Global capitalism had transformed it
and was continuing to transform it. But did the sailors notice?

"The city usually doesn't make too much of an impression on
them," Conrado says. "They can't get an impression. They're
shopping — for necessities, jeans, soap. The amenities, the
beauty of the place — they hardly notice. At most they see it
when they come into the harbour. They are more interested in
calling home, using the phones."

A number of factors contribute to this. One is the ever-grow-
ing need for security at the world's ports: security because of
threats of terrorism and because of illegal immigration. "It's not
really affecting the sailors getting ashore," Reverend Pike says.
"They get to go downtown. But they do have to be back on the
ship at night. There are security issues." And so strangers can't
get into the secure areas on Vancouver's docks; and you can only
get on a ship if you really have reason to get on it. He smiles at
me. "If you applied for a pass, they'd likely say no."

He pauses. "I've heard — I'm not sure — but I've heard that
there can be up to a $10,000 fine for the captain if a sailor doesn't
return to the ship. Some captains, I believe, make their sailors
keep their passports on the ship. So they won't run away. This
makes it difficult to go to a bank. Of course, they will have other
ID." He pauses again, choosing his words. "You see, before the

ship leaves, the captain has to get clearance from customs, immigration, which means all the sailors have to be on board."

Was this a change?

"In the past there may have been more lapses." Again he pauses. "In some countries a sailor has to put down a bond. A sum of money. They'll lose that if they jump ship. Mind you, when they're in port, when it's their time to be off, they're fairly free to go where they want."

Do they get to spend the night in the city?

"No. They have to be back by eleven pm. They all sleep on board ship. Usually they leave the ship in shifts, each shift for a specific number of hours. I suppose things have changed. For instance, there are no sailors' hostels anymore. So sailors can't just leave one ship and sign on to another. You can't go from one ship to another anymore. So that sailor's life on the streets that perhaps you used to find, it no longer exists."

Reverend Pike tells me about the expanding port, the speed at which things are now loaded and unloaded. "An extraordinary amount of cargo comes through here. People really have no idea." And CenTerm was going to expand in the next year or so by at least fifty percent. "Things have changed; and they're going to change faster. You know, years ago the cruise ships used this place. Isn't that interesting? Now the cruise ships have a thousand people on the crew," even more tightly regimented than the Russians. "We couldn't possibly serve them."

4

The bureaucracy that has sprung up to control the world's migrations, and the newer bureaucracy that has sprung up to avert terrorists: these help explain why Vancouver's sailors have become invisible. But the larger reason is the ever-increasing regimentation and industrialization of sailing. One night years ago, when I was a teenager, I came into Vancouver on an old Black Ball ferry, one that docked downtown around where Canada Place is now. I saw the city that night as if in a dream: the lit-up buildings, and the reflection of their lights on the water, seemed strange and beautiful. For the modern sailor, no doubt, that strangeness and beauty remain. But they are surface things only, mere physical facts. Beyond that the city means little: it is a place to shop, a place to make urgent phone calls and to check for e-mails. Then back to the ship.

Vancouver no longer sees the seafarers who visit it: they have disappeared. But equally, Vancouver has disappeared for the sailors. They come to it, but the city itself they no longer see. They have neither the time nor the inclination. It has become for them just another stop in a worldwide industrial corridor, just another service station along the way.

Snow Ghosts

1

For many of the years that I worked in the post office I lived in an old part of Vancouver down near the bottom of Nanaimo Street. One place I lived in the longest I've mentioned already: an apartment block that stood at the end of Wall Street where Wall runs into Powell, close to the docks. An ugly place. The halls were long, dimly lit, segmented by heavy fire doors that were always propped open. When you walked down a hall and somebody stepped out of their suite, both of you averted your eyes. People stole things, and angry notes were pinned up in the laundry room.

WHOEVER TOOK MY COTTON CABLEKNIT
SWEATER CAN RETURN IT TO THIS TABLE.

YOUR A SHIT, THIEF, AND WE KNOW
WHO YOU ARE.

The apartments themselves were the poorly designed boxes that you found everywhere in Vancouver then — tiny little kitchens and bathrooms that you could hardly turn around in, and huge living rooms and bedrooms with cheapo wall-to-wall on the floor and ugly chandeliers hanging from the stucco ceiling in the "dining room" part of the giant living room. Most people who lived in these units furnished them with furniture that would have been fine in smaller rooms, but made these huge rooms look barren and desolate.

Most of the time I was part of all this. The unit was cheap, and I liked the people and the birds and the railroad tracks and the view of the ocean. But one year a great anxiety gradually took hold of me. By the time winter came I found it hard to go out. I imagined that the other tenants in the building disliked me. If I saw Mary Willoughby in the hall in her tight corduroy jeans, I could hardly look at her. I struggled for days before getting up the courage to go to the laundry room and do my laundry. And sometimes in the afternoon, when my anxiety was at its worst, I just sat on the couch and rocked back and forth.

This was how it was with me when one night I woke suddenly from where I'd been dozing on the bed. A light filled the room that was like the light in a church. I got up from the bed and went to the window. It was snowing hard out. The concrete mass that was BC Ice and Cold Storage loomed up dark behind the curtain of falling snow. I realized what had woken me: because of the cold, the generators in the refrigerator trucks had been shut off.

The snow made a soft sound against the window. Since I had just woken up and my mind was fresh I felt a faint excitement watching it. But then the old worry and unease came creeping back. I turned on a lamp, paced back and forth, picked up pieces of fluff from the carpet. Then I stared at myself in the dark bathroom mirror.

I'd already checked the phone. It was working. It was just that no one had called. It was quarter after seven. I thought of the few people I might call, maybe go out and have dinner with. But what if they turned me down? It would be horrible to have that happen. Twice I started dialing a number; each time I stopped midway, holding the phone off the hook, motionless, thinking hard about whether it was too late to call or not, yet at the same time hearing or feeling a kind of static hiss of distraction. I was deeply lonely.

I needed to talk to someone, to look at someone. I got up and went through my books, looking for something to read.

But the books were no good. I needed something else.

2

The Dorry Market took up the ground floor of an old two-storey stucco building. Old wooden steps that already had a half-inch of snow on them led up the side of the building to the welfare apartments that were on the upper floor. The tailor's shop beside the market was dark, but even through the swirling snow I could make out the two satin dresses and the striped shirt with the big collar that Amir had hung in the window.

I opened the door with its metal 7-Up sign and went inside.

Warmth; people laughing and talking. It was more than I'd expected; and like someone coming into a surprise birth-day party who at first frowns and feels dismay, I immediately became stiff. Harry, who was blind in one eye, which made him look constantly distracted, and his wife Pauline sat behind the counter on high stools drinking whiskey out of plastic cups and talking to the four people who were seated on Dairyland crates by the door and who were also drinking whiskey. By sight at least I knew them all: Harry's friend Tak, who worked as a clerk at the local postal station; Darryl, who was the boyfriend of Harry and Pauline's daughter Anne; and Marilyn and Bella, two women from upstairs. Christmas decorations hung everywhere in the little room, coloured lights and red and green bells made of crepe paper. Forty or more Christmas cards dangled down from a piece of string that had been tacked across the wall behind the counter.

I had expected none of this. I muttered hello; then immedi-ately went into the dark, cramped, wooden rows, looking for things to buy. I picked up a box of Cheez Ritz crackers, a jar of dill pickles, a pack of McGavin's cinnamon buns. Then I went to the cooler and picked out a garlic sausage and a block of Cheddar cheese. After thinking about it a bit, I added a quart of Dairyland eggnog. Then I went to the magazines. They didn't have much, but I picked out *Time*, *Newsweek*, *Saturday Night* and *Scientific American*.

Harry rang up my things. "You want any Drum?"

"Sure. Good idea." My voice was hoarse and soft from disuse.

"Good. 'Cause then I can give you this for a Christmas present." And Harry handed me a half dozen yellow packs of Vogue cigarette papers on top of a big box of Redbird strike-anywhere matches with their dual-coloured heads.

I felt overwhelmed. "Thank you. This is terrific."

"Pull up a crate and have a drink," Harry said. He gestured to the stack of yellow and blue Dairyland crates by the door and at the same time filled a blue plastic cup half full of whiskey and handed it to me.

I sat down on a crate beside Tak and sipped the whiskey, tasting its good whiskey taste. It heated me going down. Almost immediately I felt a bit more relaxed.

Tak said, "The snow ghosts are gonna come out tonight." He nodded and took a drink.

Bella, who had a big round nose, said, "What are snow ghosts, Tak?"

"You don't know that? Snow ghosts? They live in the walls of old buildings. Where people have lived and died. Probably lots in this building."

Harry said, "Old Arlene died last year just above Amir's shop."

"Well, then her ghost'll be out tonight. When the snow is falling hard like this, snow ghosts feel at home."

"Tak, what is this horseshit you're talking about," Harry said. But Pauline smiled. "Let him talk. I'm curious. So, Tak, do they do anything when it snows?"

"Sure they do. They go out on the street. They move in the air. They go by the sides of buildings, down alleys. They go up stairs and fire escapes. They sit on the tops of telephone poles and whisper your name. You can hear them when you walk out in the snow, in the sound of the snow falling."

"Man, you're scaring us with all this," Harry said. Everyone laughed and took a drink.

Tak stared at him. "You look out that door now, you'll see snow ghosts right by the side of the store. You bet."

Darryl half stood up from his crate. "I better open the door and check."

Marilyn said, "Darryl, you leave that door shut!"

"That's right," Bella said. "The last thing we need in here is ghosts dripping down our necks."

Pauline said, "I remember when I was a kid up in the Highland Valley outside Merritt, there used to be ghosts. We had an outhouse. I used to be so afraid to go to that outhouse at night! On a cold night when there was snow on the ground and the moon was out and the wind was blowing, the ghosts would go into the outhouse and down into the hole."

Bella said, "Did anything ever happen?"

Pauline thought about it. "Well, one night I had to pee. I said to my mom — my stepmom, really — 'Mom, I don't want to go to the outhouse. Let me pee in a pot.' I was that scared that I said that! And she got angry. Because she was afraid of the ghosts, too. And because I was afraid, that made her fear get even bigger. So finally she said, 'Okay, look, go with one of your sisters.' I had nine sisters. So I ask Emily in the bunk above me to go with me. And by now I'm rocking back and forth on my bunk I gotta pee so bad."

She paused, and took a drag on her cigarette. Tak said, "You peed in the pot." We all laughed. I smiled, and sipped more whiskey and took a drag on my own cigarette.

Pauline said, "Nope. No, I didn't. We went out. We put on our parkas and slippers over our pyjamas and went outside holding hands. The wind was blowing the snow in the air. It was so cold! And the moon was out. And there in the blowing snow around the outhouse I saw a ghost."

Pauline was a practical woman, and as far as I knew she never lied. We all looked at her. Darryl said, "Come on, you did not."

"I did. Just out of the corner of my eye. Small, like a child, just slipping around the corner of the outhouse. It was a she, a little girl. I just saw her for a second. God, I was so scared. I said to Emily, 'Please Emily, come in with me.' And she did, right into the outhouse. And then I was on the icy cold hole trying to pee, and I hear a whisper: 'Help me.'"

Pauline smoked. "I couldn't look down. I had to pee. I had already started. So I peed. I peed as fast as I could. And then we got out of there and ran home and got under the covers." She paused. "And that's the story." She glanced at Harry, as if she had something more to say, then took a drag on her cigarette and stared into space, smiling then frowning.

I said, "It's a good story."

She smiled, and Harry nodded and looked out the store window at the red and blue snow falling in the neon light from the store's sign. "I never seen a ghost myself. But I had a horse who did. I think, anyway.

"This was just after I met Pauline." Harry inclined his head towards his wife. "It was right after the end of the war. I was working up at Hat Creek. At the Camerons'. We were cutting cattle out. Wet and dry, you know what I mean. We only had a few left to do. Frost on the ground in places 'cause it had froze last night and the sun was just comin' up. So: frost here, mud and slime there, and manure everywhere. Typical."

Then something invisible to Harry came into the place where he was working. The animals started to scream. The temperature dropped. For a moment Harry felt that he could see right through the chute. Nothing seemed real except the invisible thing in the air. Harry's horse, a sorrel, "a nice about eleven, twelve hundred pounds," stood straight up screaming in fright then fell backwards, so that Harry's saddle worked into his groin.

Tak grimaced. "Painful."

"It was," Harry said. "I had to go to the Lady Minto hospital down in Ashcroft to get it fixed. But I'll tell you, I'll never forget that sudden cold and how just for a second there that chute looked transparent. I've never seen animals as scared as those were. Me too."

We were silent for a while, sipping our whiskey. Then Marilyn said: "I talked to a ghost once. And I didn't even know it."

"When was that?" Bella said.

"Remember that house on Lakewood that Johnny and me and my mom used to live in? It was when we lived there. And it was in that house."

She sipped her whiskey and took a drag on her cigarette and straightened out the housecoat she was wearing over her house-dress and leaned forward. "My mom was sick then and she spent most of her time in bed in her bedroom upstairs. Well, this particular morning she'd spent all morning in bed, sleeping, I guess, and I was downstairs in the kitchen.

"I was baking bread. I used to bake bread in these various tins, round tins, narrow tins, all kinds. Took me all morning. But I like to make my own bread. It tastes better.

"Anyway. I'm working away and I hear mom in the living room. I guess she's woken up and come down. 'How's it going?' she calls out and I can hear the squeak of the rocking chair so I know she's rocking. 'Gonna feed the neighbourhood again?' She always had a sense of humour. 'Not bad. Ten loaves,' I says. 'Wanna help?'"

Marilyn paused and sipped her whiskey. Then she was silent. We all looked at her. "What?" Bella said.

"I don't know. But I think I might have felt something when I asked that question. Something . . . I don't know. But I could hear the rocker squeak, so I just kept on working. Then I said, 'So do you think ten loaves will be enough for today?' Making a joke. She didn't say anything. So I repeated it: 'Do you think ten loaves will be enough for today?'

"No answer. Well suddenly I feel cold as ice and I put down the pan I'm working with and I step into the living room and I see the rocking chair move back and forth. Jesus Christ."

Bella shuddered and put her hand over her mouth. "Oh no."

"That's right. There's nobody in it. I say: 'Mom? Where are you? Mom? Where are you, god damn it. Answer me!' Standing there in the living room like a fool, shivering and shaking."

She sipped her whiskey. "Well. Finally I went upstairs. Probably the hardest thing I ever did in my life. And there she was, lying in bed on her back. Her eyes were open and her mouth was open. Her teeth weren't in."

"Was she dead?" Darryl said.

"That's right. I called the ambulance, and then I waited outside the house for them to come. I couldn't be inside the house, not after what had happened."

Marilyn drank the last of her whiskey and smiled at us. "And that's my ghost story, and I'll swear on a stack of Bibles that every word is true."

"Well, it's a hell of a story," Harry said and everyone agreed that it was in fact pretty much the best ghost story they had heard.

3

When I left the store about twenty minutes later, it was still snowing. The snow landed with a soft brushing noise on the snow that had already fallen. That was the only sound. I felt a bit drunk, but otherwise filled with happiness. I had talked with other human beings; I was part of the world again.

Back in my apartment I sat up eating a McGavin's cinnamon bun and looking out at the snow, thinking about the things I had heard and seen: Bella with her big round nose, Harry's blind eye, Marilyn talking and leaning forward in her housedress. Sometimes when I was bored I would make small animals from paper clips and dangle them from a magnet. Now, like a giraffe, a snake, a seagull, and a pelican, all dangling one from the other, the events of the night dangled one after the other from my happiness. This was the world I lived in; and for the first time I saw that it was interesting.

I leaned forward until the bridge of my nose pressed against the window. The air was grey: BC Ice and Cold Storage showed up only as a blurred outline. I picked a single snowflake out of the millions and watched it come towards me out of the darkness, twisting and spinning. How wonderful the night had been! More had been given to me than I had expected or hoped for.

When I woke the next morning I found that the feeling of happiness I had been filled with the previous night was still with me. Something obscure had taken place in me that I had no name for.

In the process my anxiety had played itself out. I had started writing an article for the *Vancouver Postal Worker* about a recent sit-in. But I had put the article aside. It seemed hopeless. Now, even before I had a cup of coffee I picked the article up and read through it. There were things in it that were bad and I could see what they were; but there were also good things. I made my coffee and while I was drinking it I started to rewrite the article, thinking about what I had heard the previous night, giving dialogue to people, putting in bits of conversation I'd heard or thought I remembered. And — because it had also been snowing during the sit-in – the piece filled up with the luminous atmosphere of my night at the Dorry Market.

I worked quickly.

And then it was finished. Never had I written anything so easily. I folded the sheets longways and put them in the inside pocket of my sports coat.

That morning's 11 AM editors' meeting in which I was told about the changes I would have to make and during which I shouted that we didn't need communists running the *Postal Worker* I prefer not to see as part of this story. I'd rather conclude with a memory of coming back into my unit – I needed to get some gloves – and discovering that the air in the room where I'd been writing was thick with the smell of sweat.

Glavin's Progress

1

I discovered Terry Glavin late, in the mid-nineties. New Star Books had sent the *Vancouver Review* a review copy of his most recent book.

I read the book. I became excited. Acting on impulse I called up New Star's publisher, Rolf Maurer.

Rolf said that Glavin had worked as a reporter for the *Vancouver Sun*. He had covered the Native affairs beat. But management had turned against him — he had shown too much concern for Indians.

"How old was he then?"

"In his thirties."

"What happened?"

"Well. He accused the *Sun* of burying stories. So he was buried, or so I was told. The way I heard it, his desk was moved out to the new plant in Surrey when nobody else's was. He hung on for a while, then he quit."

So his books were a revenge — and a good one, I thought: three books in four years.

I read the first two books, and I could see why he and the *Sun* had quarreled. Glavin was openly political. He had an understanding of BC history which would have been too complicated for the *Sun*. And he was an idealist. The degradation of Native society that the media regularly reported on didn't appear in his work. Instead he showed an almost visionary attitude towards his subject. Reading his early books I saw Glavin fight towards a representation of BC in which our old sense of the bush as an economic trough and the Natives as degraded exotics was thrown out once and for all. In these books, the format, the point of view, even the shape of the sentences changed as Glavin battled to express an idea about BC that was completely new.

2

The first book, *A Death Feast in Dimlahamid*, came out in 1990. It was a report on the Gitskan-Wet'suwet'en people in north-central BC. Using dozens of interviews and a small library of background texts, Glavin described the people's legal and social history, their myths and ceremonies (he attended one of the death feasts), and their current situation. In particular *A Death Feast* told the story of the blockade the Natives set up near Kispiox in 1989.

The book contained good writing. Consider the following passage. It's a freezing night, three AM; Robert Jackson in his pickup truck has just pulled a huge cedar log across the road,

> where, on a normal day, a fully loaded logging truck would pass every ten minutes in an annual convoy that took 500,000 cubic meters of wood . . . out of the Kispiox valley highlands. About twenty of the young men were there already, and they stood around the blazing fire, stamped their feet on the frozen ground and tucked their cold hands deep into their pockets. . . . Wii Muugalsxw, who is the soft-spoken, forty-year-old Kispiox artist and carver Art Wilson, smiled nervously as the first logging truck showed up.

I can see that smile. As well as the men's need to take action, Glavin shows me their diffidence.

Or consider this scene. At a meeting in the Kispiox community hall, a reticent Native lawyer named Gordon Sebastian has finally started to express what concerns him:

> Everybody listened. Gordon didn't speak much at these things.
> "You know, I see our people on reserve. A good ninety per cent of the people, a good ninety per cent. They're poor ... They're very poor. And you know, I live off the backs of the poor people. I'm on the band council. I have a job because of the poor people on the reserve.
> "Sunday morning when I went to the Suskwa roadblock? There was nobody there. So I went over to the road and put up the block. I put up the blockade. No problem. One little Indian. One little Hagwilget Indian, for a couple of hours. Don't you see how strong you are? I didn't have 200 Indians there. There was just one. And you know who's been manning the roadblock? You know who's manning the roadblock now? Poor people. It's the poor people. They're living off grouse and moose meat, and whatever food we bring out. Poor people."

In just a few words an entire world.

So — good writing. But I also found problems. Glavin mixed events and stories in *A Death Feast* in a way that made it hard to sort out what was going on. I read the book carefully; but even at the end I had no clear sense of how the blockade had progressed and what its emotional and cultural dynamics had been. Glavin didn't shape his material sufficiently, didn't reach for a dramatic form. In particular he left more or less untouched the Native legends he had transcribed and which ran all through the book. They interrupted the narrative; and, with every verbal stumble included, they had no force: their strangeness and power got dissipated in the tentative way they were told.

And I found problems with Glavin's representation of character. The Natives he reported on were too often presented in an idealized manner that didn't work the way Glavin wanted it to. For one thing, in order to suggest the complexity of their background — and, perhaps, in order to ennoble them — they were given both their contemporary and their tribal names. But these tribal names belonged to ancestors going back for millenia, so it wasn't always clear whether it was the ancestor or the contemporary person who was being referred to. This confusion was deliberate; but instead of elevating the individuals so named, it depersonalized them.

Most important, Glavin didn't take the risk of providing his own insights into people. He didn't present the telling gesture, the detail of face or clothing or behaviour that would reveal character. Instead he cultivated a solemn "country" voice that at times in the sombre roll of its sentences sounded like the voice of a tribal chief on television. It was a voice and a style of presentation which kept so respectful a distance from the people Glavin wrote about that they seemed blurred, Indians moving behind an ideological scrim.

3

Glavin's next book, *Nemiah: The Unconquered Country*, came out in 1992. In some ways it was similar to *A Death Feast*. It concerned the social and legal history of a group of Native people (in this case the Nemiah Valley Indian band up in the Chilcotin, descendants of those Natives who had fought in the uprising now known as the Chilcotin War); it transcribed their stories; and it related their current fight to keep whites from eating up their land.

But I found *Nemiah* to be a different and better book than the first one. To start with, it contained expressive photographs throughout. These gave the reader a clear sense of the place and people Glavin was talking about. Equally important, it separated out the Natives' stories into boxed-off sections. Alone on the page like this, surrounded by white space, a kind of quiet emanated from them, with the result that I again and again heard a thrillingly soft, unguarded tone of voice which was unlike any voice I had ever heard before in a book. And Glavin's own style, which in *A Death Feast* had seemed newspaperman-flat, now showed a little more of the vision that moved him. In particular, he had found a way to suggest how the country voice, the Native voice, could be eloquent and telling. A subtle thing; but flatness now sometimes turned into quietness and at moments I sensed the man full of emotion behind the cautious text.

I still found problems. Glavin had again bitten off more than he could chew. History, ethnography, personal memoir and current-affairs reportage all milled about in the text, getting in each other's way. It was hard to find a strong story, and after a while I stopped trying. Also, while you could now hear what Glavin was up to with his "country" voice, chunks of the book seemed laboured.

4

But I saw all this only after I received Glavin's third book in the mail and read it in one sitting.

That book, *A Ghost in the Water*, was about a fishing trip Glavin had taken with his friends Marvin Rosenau and Nick Basok to catch a Fraser River white sturgeon. And while here, too, the writing mixed various kinds of text — history, bio-ethnography — everything came together. The book moved fast; the prose was nervous and intense. And the mood it sustained astonished me. Glavin's writing now evoked a physical darkness, the darkness of the grey and darker-grey skies that for weeks on end drop rain onto the Fraser. By the end of the book I had felt the black strangeness of the river's forests, the hissing life of its surface. Making vivid use of poetry and historiography, Glavin's text ended up presenting a vision of BC that wasn't like anything I had read before.

Three things helped him do this. First, he now owned his prose, writing sentences that were unafraid of complexity and had no trace of a false vernacular. Second, he had learned how to artfully mix various kinds of texts. Eloquent black-and-white photos, Native legends, history and biology were all seamlessly woven into the book. Partly because *A Ghost in the Water* was so short, less than a hundred pages, the fishing trip that provided its story stayed clear. I knew when Glavin was picking up one textual thread and dropping another, and I felt confident he would get where he wanted to go. Finally, the assemblage of facts and stories that Glavin had put together now had the interest of personal myth. Like his fishing companions, Glavin had grown up "within shouting distance" of the Fraser; and in *A Ghost in the Water*, quoting Diana Hartog's "poetic bestiary" ("Twenty feet long and gunmetal grey, the sturgeon swim among schools of sunken locomotives — old steam engines which have flung themselves off the end of the line, to lie tilted on their sides, breathing deeply through their gills") – in *A Ghost in the Water*, he had created something like his own river legend:

> I had never found a sturgeon of any size on the end of any line I ever cast, but I was dimly aware of the rumours. Giant, twenty-foot water monsters dwelt in the depths of the river. They fell within a childhood taxonomy that included the Sasquatch, the ghosts that haunted the house on Russell Avenue, terrifying swamp animals from the Burnaby flats, and the creatures that lurked in long-forgotten tunnels under the streets of New Westminster.

Street names, place names, fragments of old newspaper stories from papers like the *New Westminster Columbian*, moody black and white photos, Native legends — which now had the power of stories like "Hansel and Gretel" — it all evoked a vision of BC that ran strongly against the sunny, history-denying vision most British Columbians grow up with. There were no Okanagan apples the size of trucks here, no images of shining conifers in postcard Kodachrome that were supposed to make you feel like the lord of the universe. It was as if the black shadow that Glavin saw on BC had become for him a source of visions — had fined him down and given his prose life.

5

The next year Glavin returned to journalism with *Dead Reckoning*, a look at BC's fishing industry. Journalism; yet the book also contained extraordinary scholarship — the list of "sources" at the back made up six pages of tiny print: hundreds of books and articles. That same year, and more remarkably to me, he published *This Ragged Place*, a collection of nine essays that dealt in particular with the lies, preconceptions and racist paranoia that all through the 1990s had characterized the BC media's presentation of Native concerns.

In these essays Glavin outlined a story that went to the heart of BC's colonial structure. If you wanted to know who had power in British Columbia and how little scruples mattered to them in defending that power, you only had to read "From the Old Rice Mill to Annieville Drift," in which Glavin documented the hysteria that grabbed the province because of Ottawa's Aboriginal Fishing Strategy agreement with the Fraser River Natives.

Glavin starts with a date: August 21, 1992. The BC Supreme Court is visited by an industry lobby group, the Fisheries Council of BC. Its request: scrap the aboriginal fishing strategies deal.

"Between them," Glavin writes, FCBC members "accounted for almost the entire production and distribution of BC salmon products. They came to court arm in arm with the Pacific Fisherman's Alliance ... and with the BC Wildlife Federation, the Steelhead Society of British Columbia, and the United Fishermen and Allied Workers Union."

These people had authority on their side. They were respectable. The Natives weren't. And so the media listened attentively as their lawyers outlined a terrifying scenario: "an ecological cataclysm had occurred in the Fraser River ... 1.2 million Fraser River sockeye had 'disappeared' between Mission Ridge and their spawning grounds. Indian poachers were to blame."

The *Province* and the *Vancouver Sun*, along with BCTV News, swallowed and regurgitated it all. Stories about 1992's "poaching" and "missing fish" continued on an almost daily basis well into 1993.

Alarm spread. On February 27, 1993, 2,500 protesters turned up at a fisheries survival rally in Victoria. In coastal towns like Campbell River Native and non-Native kids were reported fighting. And in early summer of '93 Dennis Brown — secretary-treasurer of the fishermen's union and a key spokesman for the Fisheries Survival Coalition — told the *Vancouver Sun* that if there was violence between Indians and whites fishing in the Fraser River, it would not be his fault, it would be the government's fault, and he would hold the federal government "solely responsible."

But here's the thing. None of it was true. The Native fishery hadn't expanded. The salmon available hadn't dwindled. There was no "biological disaster" on the Fraser in 1992. In fact, as Glavin notes, it was quite a good year, the catch being the highest in that year in the fish cycle since the forties.

And there was no increase in the tribal-share of that catch. Indeed, the beneficiaries of this good year weren't the Natives (who then, as now, got about 5 percent of the catch), but "the companies that make up the coastal monopoly and the seiners in Juan de Fuca Strait."

A remarkable story. And Glavin told it eloquently, staying low-key and documenting his points. He let his readers feel indignation for themselves.

As I read the essays collected in *This Ragged Place* I got a sense of Glavin going about his work: talking to people, meditating on BC's landscape and how it has shaped our ways of thinking and looking. In the course of the book he travelled from the Yellowhead Pass down to the coast, to Finn Slough, to Liumchen Canyon off the Chilliwack River, to the downtown Vancouver offices of the Council of Forest Industries, to Dog Creek and Alkali Lake, to 100 Mile House, to Alexis Creek off Highway 20 in the Chilcotin, and to Gitwinksihlkw,

a vast and barren plain of jumbled and broken volcanic

rock, the kind of landscape that might belong on some distant planet, except there is a slippery mud road through the middle of it and a line of telephone poles stretches off into the distance and disappears into the horizon. The road went on and on in this way, through sleet and rain, until it became possible, between the swipes of wiper blades across a muddy windshield, to make out an intersection in the distance. At the crossroads, a sign pointed to the north.

Reading the book, I felt I was seeing a BC that had never appeared before in print. The essays had many good qualities. But I most valued their sense of emotion reined in by sobriety. Glavin exposed the pretense that here in BC we have developed an advanced society, progressive and cutting-edge. In the words of Vancouver art critic Robert Linsley, he showed that "what we learn from our local history is that the spirit of the province is dark, oppressive and wounded." His gravity of tone reflected that recognition.

6

In 1998 Glavin was asked by the *Globe and Mail* to be its west coast correspondent. Around the same time he was appointed to the Pacific Fisheries Resource Conservation Council. More important, he was busy soliciting material for, and editing, an extraordinary series of books about British Columbia which may end up being his finest achievement. Each of the Transmontanus books (of which *A Ghost in the Water* was the first) ran to about a hundred pages; each came out in paperback, with a visually rich cover and a nearly square format; each contained photographs and other graphic images; and each presented an idiosyncratic, personal look at BC which nonetheless proved to be part of a larger vision, a piece, you might say, of a mosaic depicting the province that was like nothing that had appeared before.

Appropriately, I discovered these books outside of Vancouver. I was travelling in the Interior for the first time in over twenty

years, travelling the gravel roads that extended across the Fraser
River into the Chilcotin. And one day I drove into Lillooet, a
small logging town just east of the Coast Range whose Native
moms and empty dirt lots down by the railroad tracks seemed
to sum up the landscape I had been passing through. There, at a
gift store that was having a sale, I bought three books that were
part of the Transmontanus series.

Later that afternoon, at the Cayoosh Campground down near
the Fraser, I flipped through them. It was sunny and windy,
wind lifting the pages of my books. A fine dust blew onto the
blue-painted wood of the picnic table into which someone had
gouged PARTY TIL YOUR PANTS DROP. A woman sitting
in a folding chair in the campsite across from me shouted into
the blowing dust: "Ginger, do your postcards like I told you! You
goddamn little bugger!" And it was in this riverside campsite,
with the dust blowing, that I started to read Theresa Kishkan's
Red Laredo Boots.

I read it right through. It contained thirteen short personal
essays. They were written in an intimate, factual style and often
took the form of diary entries or impressions from a journal.
And because of their lightness of touch, because they drew me
in not with soul-baring but with a careful display of the details
of trips Kishkan had taken, on page after page I thought: I've
been there.

As I read I became excited. Travelling on the Interior's gravel
roads, with the dust rising and the sharp stones banging against
the underside of the car, I had found that landscape which for
each of us is the most magical: the landscape of childhood. And
Kishkan had seen that too. So I projected myself into her book,
discovering in it something I had never before encountered in
print. Kishkan wrote about travelling on the great Highland
Valley road, and I remembered what I had felt driving that same
road four days earlier — how in the nearly perfect silence when
I stopped the car the sunlight had seemed to come from another
time, and how as I descended into Ashcroft the canyons and
desert mesas below had stretched to the rim of the earth. I had
stopped and got out for a look; and just as the bush towns of

north-west Alberta had appeared as little models — small, circumscribed, pregnant with the magic of miniaturization, there so far below us — when my dad and I had descended the hairpin turns leading down out of the Rockies, so the world I saw below me as I looked down at Ashcroft seemed like a model made of painted papier-mache.

No doubt the thrill I felt was disproportionate. Kishkan's essays were modest; small things. Yet as I read them, that sense of possibility came over me which I suppose for every writer is the real beginning of a work. I thought: I could do this. Here was a literary person, a modern person, who had travelled through the same BC that I had. I recognized a lot in her book; in particular I recognized the haunted tone that sounded all through *Red Laredo Boots*, as if Kishkan had come at almost the last moment when this landscape commensurate with her sense of wonder was still available.

7

Over the next few days, travelling in the Big Bar country, I saw that Kishkan's feeling of belatedness was something *Red Laredo Boots* shared with the second of the three books I'd bought. *High Slack* was a difficult book, tense and shifting. Its author, Judith Williams, a visual artist, had left the coast at Bute Inlet to travel past the Homathko Icefield up to the mouth of the Homathko River — a journey that retraced in prose Robert Homfray's 1861 trip up the same inlet.

A mind-altering journey; and at times it warped Williams's language as she attempted to recreate the glare of perception. But she had found amazing photographs to illustrate her text, and as is sometimes the case with pictures that hold a superabundance of reality, a few carried unintended meanings. It transfixed me, for instance, to see alone on a page the great strange picture of the mouth of the Homathko, while on the facing page Williams listed the food she had found in a cookhouse trailer: "pizzas, paté , cheese of many kinds, and cookies (peanut butter, chocolate chip) . . . Nanaimo and date bars, a dozen pies (pecan, apple, raisin and cherry), and Jello (red, yellow and green)."

How that juxtaposition of dark landscape and brightly-coloured food spoke to me! When I was 21 — two years after I had returned to Vancouver from Texas — I had worked near Port Hardy as a line cutter. And contemplating Williams's juxtaposition of text and picture it all came back: how in that Peruvian world of work and mud and hillsides so steep we had dropped in the fog like mountain climbers, we had assuaged ourselves with helicopter-loads of food — food being the great pleasure of bush work. I remembered how on the one day when it was finally raining too hard to work — a day of paleolithic relaxation — Hal and Barry and I had eaten and slept all afternoon, going back and forth in the mud to the cook tent and occasionally glancing at the surrounding bush, which in the rain carried all the primeval power of the picture in *High Slack*.

8

But of the three books I became most excited by *Chiwid*. Its author, Sage Birchwater, had moved out to Tatla Lake in 1977. He had run a trapline and taken up journalism, writing about the Chilcotin for the *Williams Lake Tribune* and the *Coast Mountain News* of Bella Coola. He had gotten the chance to meet some of the characters of the Chilcotin, and he had started to record their stories.

Many of these stories were about Chiwid — birth name Lillie Skinner. Chiwid had been badly beaten by her husband when she was young, and she had spent the rest of her life living in the open. Because of this she had become a legend in the Chilcotin. As with most legends the stories told about her were contradictory and multiple. Chiwid could see like a coyote; her eyesight was poor. She seemed happy to many people, but in front of others her face stiffened with fear. In winter she slept under the snow.

Some of the stories might not have been true. It didn't matter. The interviews overwhelmed me. A world I didn't know about opened up. Once again a place and a people that had been unhallowed by language were being brought to life at almost the last possible moment. I was especially struck by the interviews with the Natives. So strange, their language; and so pungent. The simplest details startled me; it was as if I was tasting hotsprings water for the first time, or eating soapberries.

This, for instance, from Baptiste Elkins, who had married Chiwid's half-sister Madeline Palmantier. His first wife had come from Ulkatcho Village, and after her death, he and Madeline had continued to live in Anahim Lake:

> First time I see Chiwid, at Eagle Lake when I was a kid. Across the river at Eagle Lake Henry's. Chiwid and his mother, he come around a little bit. They stay in a smokehouse.
>
> Chiwid's mother don't talk. His name Loozap. He don't talk. He talk on his hand. He make a lot of kid, that old woman. Chiwid and Johnny Robertson, Scotty and the youngest one I been married to. Loozap lived at Eagle Lake too . . .
>
> We been looked after Loozap at Anahim Lake before he passed away. We can't do nothing. He can't eat and call nurse for him. Nurse can't do nothing for him too. He said: "I'm going to die anyway," he said. He can't do nothing for one week. Can't go toilet. No.
>
> We bury him at Anahim Lake, Loozap. Some kind of Hunlin family.

A strange voice, a voice from another world. But it evoked everything. As I read, it was as if the whole of the Chilcotin plateau had evaporated into the air then condensed onto the pages as a precipitate that smelled of grass and dry dust.

And it was all so close! The world in *Chiwid*, in *High Slack*, in *Red Laredo Boots* — from Vancouver it was just over the mountains. A kind of psychic membrane separated my home place from the one in these books. I could pass through it; and when

I did I seemed to walk in a larger world, a gigantic world, really, whose inhabitants appeared vivid in a way that people in Van-couver didn't. A flippant person might have called them charac-ters; and he would have been right. To a degree increasingly rare in the city, the meaning of people's lives here found expression in narrative. What mattered was a person's duration in time, the things he had seen and done. This was why as I travelled in the Interior it more and more came to seem like a storybook place. However wretched a person's life might seem to an outsider, it could have a meaningful shape in his own eyes and the eyes of others because over the course of the years that life became a ser-ies of stories. And one person's stories interlaced with another's; so that if you talked to the right person at the right time you could get a sense that all the stories of the Interior plateau made up one story in the end.

9

For the past few years Glavin has been working on a large book. In 2005 I sent him an e-mail asking him to describe it. I asked for a brief précis; he promptly emailed me back a sort of poem:

> As for the latest book (if I ever get the damn thing done), it's now tentatively titled *The Last Giants in the River of the Black Dragon, and Other Stories from the Age of Extinc-tion*. [It would eventually be published as *Waiting for the Macaws and Other Stories*.]
>
> It's eight chapters, each set in a different part of the world. I say eight, but really there's a lengthy prologue, set in the village of Tuamgraney in County Clare, and a long epilogue set at the temple of Kali in Calcutta; in between there are six chapters: "A Fish," "A Lion," "A Whale," "A Flower," "A Mermaid," "A World."

His e-mail went on to describe the various chapters. They evoked a cosmopolitanism that was new to Glavin but that none-theless sounded convincing. Still, it was Glavin's vision of BC –

so fiercely fought for; and so original! – that continued to impress me; and as I contemplated his e-mail I remembered once more an event I had thought of when I had first read *A Ghost in the Water.*

It involved Doane Gregory, a tall, handsome man and former cowboy whom I'd met through Kevin Williams of Raincoast Books. Doane worked now as a photographer and as a shooter of stills for the film industry in Vancouver. But when he was in his twenties he had cowboyed in the BC Interior, in particular in the Hat Creek Valley, near where Harry of the Dorry Market had worked.

Harry was Native. And one day, thinking about him, I asked Doane: "What were the Natives like when you were working on the ranches?"

It was a confused question; I knew that as I asked it. I was after much more than my words expressed. Really, I was asking Doane what his life had been like in those days.

Another person might have misunderstood me. But Doane heard what I was saying. He was silent for a moment, sipping his beer (we were drinking Coronas in the kitchen of his West Vancouver house; outside the open patio doors we could hear the traffic on the Upper Levels Highway), then he told me this story:

"This happened one of the times when the Gang Ranch changed hands — I can't remember which time — but it was then. There's a whole passel of the Rosette family, who are old-time Natives, cowboys, up there. And Willy Rosette was, I believe, the cow boss of the Gang Ranch at the time. An excellent cattleman, an excellent horseman. Natives are often an incredible asset to an operation, but they still do things in their own way and they just drive most white guys up the wall. They'll listen to something the boss has to say, and they'll kind of just go and do it the way they do it — it's usually for the better, but maybe it'll take a bit longer. But it's really very different.

"Anyway, I think it was one of the Rosette kids who was working on the ranch who was not getting on with the owner. And the owner fired him, in full sight of all these people at the main ranch, which is kind of like a town — there's a lot of buildings there, it's a real hub.

"So the next morning, the owner walks into the cookhouse — a big, old-fashioned cookhouse where the cowboys eat — and this kid was sitting there at the table, having breakfast. And the owner said, '*What* are you doing here. I *fired* you. You are *out* of here. You will never work on this place again.'

"And the kid said —" And here Doane made his voice small and timid and yet also assertive, so that I could completely see the boy — "'Well . . . you know . . . you fired me . . . But I was born here . . . You know . . . . . . I live here.'"

I live here. In *A Ghost in the Water*, Terry Glavin had said exactly this. A journalist had turned himself into a poet in order to tell me where he lived. He wanted me to see the place; he wanted me to see its history, its geography and its people, with no dimension of myth or legend left out. And if I write about him at length, I do so because before him I had never seen any BC writer do that. It suggested to me that things were changing in our literature, and that from now on these changes would have to be taken into account.

The Crosses

1

Sometimes we have ideas about phenomena that take years before they find a form or even the beginning of a form. So it was with me and the concept of Native art.

2

On the coast, in a reversal of the usual winter pattern, something like a drought had set in. And about a week after I came back from my second and more melancholy trip across the prairies, with the sun shining and the blackberry bushes covered with dust in the vacant lots downtown (something that made the air seem even colder than it was), I saw in a window of the Hotel Vancouver a soapstone carving of an Inuit hunting a seal that was exactly like the small carving I'd bought for my mom when I was fifteen.

I stared at it. Every detail was the same. Then, reacting, maybe, or building on the disillusionment I'd felt in Alberta's great Glenbow Museum and afterward in the small towns and reserves of Saskatchewan and Manitoba, I started to look in other store windows that displayed Native art — stores on Georgia Street and then, later that afternoon, on Granville Street on the south side of the Granville Bridge.

I recognized it all. None of it had changed. I had noticed this before, or half-noticed it; but now the Native art in the store windows looked like tourist shop stuff, stuff that hid what was going on. And while I was looking in the window of an expensive gallery on Granville near Broadway, standing in shadow with the winter sun shining onto the street not far from the sidewalk's edge, I realized that this tourist shop art signaled a degradation so widespread I had lived my whole life without noticing it.

All around me people were shopping. They looked well-off; this was a well-off part of town. Most were young. A couple walked towards me. They wore the clothes that were just starting to become popular: hiphugger pants on the young woman (blond, smooth-faced, in her late twenties), and on the wide-shouldered, lantern-jawed man a plain poplin jacket, like a service station jacket, with script on its left upper pocket mimicking the name that would have been on the jacket his had been modelled after. A sophisticated style; and the bland faces and good haircuts of these young people, different from the faces and haircuts I had seen on my travels, sharpened the feeling of shame I felt, looking in that window.

3

That afternoon dark clouds gathered and a cold wind blew, bending the branches of the acacias outside my apartment. With my pack not yet unpacked and with all the windows open but still feeling stuffy and closed in, I tried to relate my disillusionment (but *disillusionment* isn't right; it was more than that and included a sense of discovery) to the book I was reading, an essay by Claude Lévi-Strauss on the ceremonial masks of Canada's west coast Natives.

The book contained photographs of these masks. As I read, I kept looking at them. I tried to see in them the radiant skeleton of meaning that Lévi-Strauss had found. (I also kept looking at them, I realize now, because with their recessed or stalk-like eyes, they had something of the cyborg quality that had so fascinated my friend Ronny Ballard and me in Allenby Landing when we were in our early teens reading comic books and science fiction.)

Lévi-Strauss had concentrated on two kinds of mask. One kind was light in colour, had protruding, stalk-like eyes, a gaping mouth out of which hung a carved tongue, and a trimming of stiff, upright, light-coloured feathers; the other kind was dark in colour, had deeply recessed eyes, a pursed mouth, and a trimming of limp brown hair. Noticing that these two kinds of masks seemed to be in "symmetrical opposition" to each other, Lévi-Strauss had made a decision: he had decided that the masks' physical features must have been determined by a system. He had further decided that the significance of these features couldn't be understood until the system itself was understood. Then he had asked this question: Could we "perceive, between the origin myths for each type of mask, transformational relationships homologous to those that, from a purely plastic point of view, prevail among the masks themselves?"

A hard question. But sitting there in my apartment with the winter rain at last starting to fall, his book engrossed me.

The objects in the Hotel Vancouver windows had been presented as art. But these masks weren't art. Lévi-Strauss, I realized when I was two-thirds of the way through his book, hadn't stood me in front of them and asked me to contemplate them as if they were. To have done so, he had made clear, would have been to ignore everything important about the masks. Instead he'd shown me that every one of the masks' features was determined by a system of myths and uses, and that explaining these features wasn't a matter of giving me the "meaning" of the masks but rather of making the masks intelligible.

In a way it was simple, what he had done. He had done with the masks what you would do with a traditional wedding dress if you were asked to explain it to a Tibetan teenager, say. You would tell her that the dress had a ceremonial use only, that it wasn't worn every day; you would explain that its physical features got their significance from this ceremonial use, that its white colour, for instance, derived its impact from a system of colours in which white stood for virginity, black for mourning; you would explain the veil and the bride's bouquet and you would maybe try to mimic something of the occasion on which the dress was worn. But you wouldn't treat the dress as a work of art and attempt to express what it "meant" to you.

4

In early January the sunshine returned. The things that I had seen on my travels stayed with me. They didn't dissipate; they weren't replaced by the ordinary events of my life.

By mid-January I had fallen into the habit of walking downtown on the bright chilly weekends and spending time in the library of the Vancouver Art Gallery. After two or three hours in there reading, I'd go outside onto the street, smoke, and watch a couple of Native carvers who sat bent over their blocks of wood on the sidewalk outside where Duthie Books used to be.

They sat on the sidewalk like beggars. They worked slowly, keeping their heads down, not looking up at the people who walked past. Slowly they chipped at the blocks of wood with their knives, turning them into crude totem poles. They sat in a litter of chips. No one bought the things they were making. It was hard to look at them. They embarrassed me; I never watched them for long.

Felicity, the librarian, a woman of noticeable reserve, wore long dresses and scarves. When I asked her a question her eyes widened and she shivered or trembled slightly. One day I said: "What d'you think about the carvers out on the sidewalk?"

That small tremble. "What do you mean?"

"Those two Indian guys that are working on the corner."

"I know the two you mean. Do you mean, what do I think of their work?"

"Sort of."

"Sort of?"

"Yeah, sort of." For a minute I didn't know what else to add. Then I said: "Do you think it's art?"

"Aha. So that's it."

"Well, do you?"

Kwagewlth Dzonokwa mask.

Kwagewlth Xweixwei mask.

(MILWAUKEE PUBLIC MUSEUM #80616)

"No."

"What is it then?"

She smiled. "You're interrogating me."

"I'm trying to figure something out."

She asked me what I was trying to figure out, and I wasn't sure how to answer her. Finally I said: "I guess what I want to know is, how does an artwork differ from an artifact?"

She thought about it for a long time. I had started leafing through a book when she said: "An artwork shows — deliberately — the trace or mark of an individual temperament. An ego. And it doesn't have any use."

"Is that it?"

"I think so."

My question must have intrigued her. A half hour or so later, while I was bent over an issue of Artforum, she came up to me and whispered, "There's something else. An artwork has a relationship to art history. It's a kind of research or inquiry. It shows an individual talent contesting art history or in some way coming to terms with it."

"What about a Haida mask?"

"No, I don't think so."

I thought then of the Native carvers sitting on the sidewalk in their jeans and ball caps, the caps and their long hair covering up their faces. I thought of the tourists standing above them and smiling down at them; or else glancing at them with a small grimace and walking on.

Why hadn't I seen this before?

As I finished Lévi-Strauss back at home I sometimes stared at a flyer I had recently picked up advertising a public auction of NATIVE INDIAN ART & ARTIFACTS. I noticed its familiar names — Bill Reid and Robert Davidson — and subjects: bear, hunter, seal, raven mask. The carvers on the sidewalk; and now this. What was going on here, with this listing of aboriginal objects as if they were farm implements?

If the objects were art, I thought — art in Felicity's sense, the product of art history meeting an individual talent — then why were they being sold like this? Other artworks made in Vancouver weren't sold this way. This was how Aztec things were sold in Mexico; it was how things made by the aboriginal people were sold in Australia.

No. These objects — Mexican, Australian, Western Canadian — weren't art at all but stereotyped artifacts that were produced in great quantities and were in each case the product of cultures that had suffered degradation.

So what were the buyers looking for? A token of that degradation that would give them the secret, barely conscious pleasure of comparing their situation to the one that produced the object? An exoticism, so that they could feel simultaneously sophisticated and primitive? Both, most likely, I thought, with one thing impossible to untangle from the other.

Because wasn't it true, I thought, that tribal artifacts had an *innocence* which art works by necessity lacked? Whether you were looking at a mask, an Iranian rug, a Hell's Angels jacket or a wedding dress, you noticed that no matter how striking the objects were they lacked that ability to look directly back at you that you immediately recognized in a work of art. You sensed their innocence — their vulnerability to stereotyping — because you saw their typicality, the fact that they weren't the product of individual introspection but rather of the mythology of a tribe.

In fact, I thought, the more you immersed yourself in an artifact the more subject matter you found. Not "meaning" — subject matter. To give this subject matter its due, you needed to present the artifact in a context that made it intelligible; and only the museum had the means to do so. To walk in an art gallery's white space around Dzonokwa masks or Hell's Angels jackets with their distinctive lettering and then produce comments of appreciation — that was fatuous. Only when you started to look at objects like this as something other than art could you start to see them.

Or so I thought. But even as I thought it, I knew I was missing something.

5

Over the next couple of years my ideas on Native art began to seem inadequate. Other things did too. I had started a magazine, the *Vancouver Review*; but I was still a country boy, someone who had spent most of his adult life in the penitential environment of the post office; and like a con I hadn't entirely grown up.

And now the magazine was consuming me. One evening, after a particularly bad meeting when I had been shouting and someone had told me to calm down, I was lying on my couch with my arms tightly crossed on my chest, feeling a self-loathing so extreme my body was rigid.

Sharon sat on the couch with me. After a while she said, "Maybe you should go out of town again. You've been saying you want to."

I said nothing.

"You can't go on like this. This is no good."

I lay there silent for a while. Finally I said, "I'm afraid to start."

"Well, sure."

And so once more I headed out. On a grey Sunday morning in late April, feeling deeply melancholy, with rain falling so that the cherry blossoms lay like wet snow on the sidewalk, I left Vancouver.

I wasn't sure where I was going. Turning onto the freeway, uncertainty ballooned in me. But by the time I reached Hope the sun had come out; and when I stopped to piss near Spences Bridge and smelled the dry sunlit air and saw the bar of sun on the river I felt something close to exaltation. Everything around me — above all the silence and the dry, perfumed air — spoke of my childhood; and inside me a ribbon of images started to unspool.

That evening I stopped in Cache Creek. I rented a room in a cinderblock motel that had cartoon images of Tweety and Sylvester painted on it. It was a beautiful evening; after supper I opened my door. Outside, black storm clouds were gathering above desert hills brilliant in the last sun.

I clicked on a show on BC's Knowledge Network. "Gwaii Haanas," it was called. Evocative music played — something hypnotic. A Haida mask filled the lower right of the screen. Behind it, cloudy skies billowed, ocean thundered on a thickly forested beach.

I saw right away that the mask was superimposed on the land-scape. But then — maybe because I was away from the rut of habit and maybe because outside the door rain had started to fall, rain I could smell and could see, brilliant as white diamonds in the desert sun — maybe for these reasons I realized that the mask was meant to *stand for* the complex clouds, the tangled forest. And at that point I saw that the mask on the TV screen was being presented to me not as an artifact or as an art object, but as a symbol.

And with that, everything I had so far thought about the masks was turned upside down. They had another power, I realized, a power that the very capitalism that had marginalized them was now making use of. I saw — and standing in the doorway, excited, it now seemed so obvious — I saw that this power was bound up with the political rising-up of the Natives.

For years the artifacts of Canada's aboriginal peoples had been prized for their authenticity. They had retained their object status; it was their thingness that had counted about them. They hadn't entered the circuit of modern capitalist culture and become symbols. And so they had been static, lacking the flu-idity, the easy ability to adapt and change, that contemporary images had.

But now — and how clear it was, now that I could see it! — now the artifacts produced by Canada's Native peoples had burst free of this constraint of thinghood and become the source of a flood of images that lent themselves perfectly to political use.

The drum; the pole with the thunderbird wings; the black and red Haida face: they were everywhere, part of BC's visual culture. With their simplicity and strong forms they had an iconic power that easily matched that of the red head on a Chicago Bulls jacket or the red and white Coca-Cola logo.

And people recognized this. Everyone could feel the force of these images. The technological revolution that had led images to be reproduced everywhere for essentially commercial reasons had now gone to work on the artifacts of aboriginal cultures and transformed them into vivid and powerful signs. Standing in the doorway, smelling the newly wet dust, I remembered things I had seen on my travels but only partly taken in: images on the mastheads of Indian newspapers, on T-shirts worn by Native kids; and I remembered the $1,500 black and red dresses designed by Robert Davidson and sold in Sergio Leone back in Vancouver.

That night I walked in the rain down Highway 97 to the Husky restaurant. I felt a need for company; and in the crowded Husky, hearing through the open door the trucks hissing by on the wide highway, I looked around, reflecting on what I had discovered.

Drawings of eagles and cowboys hung on the walls. Beside me at the counter an old man wearing a grey cardigan and a black cowboy hat handled his cigarette. I noticed tourists, drunks from the Oasis Hotel across the highway, two teenagers — and a fat man and his fat wife, both in shorts, both eating strawberry shortcake with whipped cream. The young wife, her fat legs spread apart, her stomach in its T-shirt a kind of sack or bag hanging over her pudenda, ate with her face only inches above her food.

I was in the Interior, in the world of my childhood; and I felt I had penetrated it. Sipping my coffee, smoking, listening ("Darling, you can have the biggest piece of pie we got," I heard the waitress say), I lined up my thoughts. Then I got out a pen. Scribbling fast, I started to make notes on my placemat. The scribbled words only abstractly represented what I felt and thought; but still they excited me.

All through the western world regions and cities are engaged in a life-or-death struggle to be noticed by the planetary culture, to be found attractive, significant, inter-

esting. In this attempt to be noticed, the tourist trade is of
the utmost importance. And what tourists want is a "real"
place, something different from the malls and cable TV
back home. They want that cafe where you can smell bitter
cigarettes and even more bitter coffee, that cobbled street,
that open-air market, that indigenous landscape, that feeling of "history," that little shop where you can buy Peruvian sweaters and authentic things made of brass. And in
city after city, as governments become desperate for the
tourist dollar, even the thinnest legends of a past and a
place are being shaped into material spaces, ad campaigns,
posters and objects that tourists can respond to.

It's the same everywhere. In England local governments feverishly play up the past, with its pubs and wind-
ing streets; in Italy ad campaigns mingle *la dolce vita* and
Michelangelo; in Australia it's the outback and visions at
Ayers Rock; and here in Supernatural BC, extending right
into this Husky with its drawings on the walls of eagles and
cowboys, it's the dream of a Native past in harmony with
nature, a dream that takes into account an overwhelming
landscape — dark islands rising out of the rain, oceans
alive with whales, primordial forests, range after range of
mountains.

An abstract. But like a fisherman's net it held a catch.

6

Crossing the highway next morning in the cold wind and brilliant sun, I went over to the Oasis Hotel to get a paper. A fat
woman and her fat daughter — so much obesity in the country!
— were reading the *Province*; with their bulk, they comman-
deered the entire rack of books and magazines.

I tried to edge around them; the daughter elbowed me.

"Excuse me," I said.

She sized me up. She was big. She was about ten years old. She
was sullen, mimicking her mom. She didn't move.

I became afraid of her. Then I edged in. She didn't budge. I pushed; and, pushing, unable to get at the *Globe*, with my shoulder pressed hard against the ten-year-old girl's immovable arm, I started flipping through a tourist's book, *The Elders Are Watching.*

It was a picture book; normally I wouldn't have looked at it. But after "Gwaii Haanas," flipping through it, I noticed the same juxtapositon of landscape and Native artifact, culminating in a painting of Vancouver in slanting rain, and, faintly visible in that rain, the ghosts of old totem poles.

So here it was again. Looking at the picture I realized that products like this had become so ubiquitous that if you lived in BC you hardly noticed them. Everywhere was this superimposition of landscape and aboriginal artifact, the one supposed to evoke the other.

And it worked! Even pressed against the big girl, I could see it. Look at a pole, and BC was summoned up. British Columbia: it was a dream made up of grey seas dotted with black-green islands, mist, tall cedars, waterfalls pouring from the impenetrable jungle on the north sides of mountains — and, of course, flying above that waterfall, a brown and white eagle, straight out of Davidson.

A dream. But without such dreams a place hardly exists. The old racist images still lingered here in the Oasis — the fat woman and her daughter had started to look through a turntable rack of postcards that included images of naked Indian girls and sad-eyed Indian kids. But a few days later in Merritt, crossing the street at the Coldwater Hotel with two Native men wearing big hats and faded jeans worn ripped at the bottoms over their cowboy boots, I went out of the hot sun into a drugstore; and there, on the counter's glass surface, beside the Maybelline and Revlon products, I saw pieces of the new idea: little totem poles, miniature masks, cedar boxes, dreamcatchers with feathers hanging from them — a cornucopia of objects made in China and Hong Kong, each contributing its tiny part to the dream vision of the place.

Once again that startled recognition. So much had happened to the civilization I'd grown up in for these objects to be here. I went outside and stood for a moment squinting against the intense sun; and at the end of the block I saw something that seemed connected in a way almost painfully ironic to what I had just seen in the drugstore.

About ten Natives, some drinking from a jug of wine, were sitting or standing near a lamp post in the parking lot of the new shopping centre. This was their place, the place where they felt at ease. And that day, tired after a night of poor sleep, with the hard sun shining and the wind blowing, I felt at ease too, sitting with them.

One of the people I sat with on the curb, a woman with a large dark head, turned and looked at me with drunken eyes that for a moment caught my own. She smiled with embarrassment. "Hi. It's a hot day, isn't it," she said.

"It is."

"Well — have a good day."

"You too."

I smoked and looked around. The kids walking by (Native kids as well as white) didn't look twice at me or the people I sat with. Yet it was BC's Native people and their ancestors, I thought, who had given the province its most important cultural export.

An idea or set of ideas can seem small at first, then grow and grow. Now an idea about Native culture that had hardly registered when I was a boy was altering Canada's vision of itself.

7

The near-desert plateau which contains the Ashcroft Reserve stretches south to the highway and north to the Thompson River. A totem pole stands in front of the band office. The Ashcroft Band hadn't known totems in the past; but poles were now a sign of Native culture throughout BC, and I recognized the change it stood for.

That day a hot wind blew. I had received permission to visit the graveyard; and as I walked out to it, licking my lips in the dry wind to moisten them, I felt I was crossing a warground on which ghosts still ran.

Springing out of the dry dirt, knee-high bunchgrass and grey-ish-green sage bent to the wind. Only the barbed-wire fence circling the cemetery separated it from the rest of the plateau.

The hot late-afternoon sun splashed blinding pools of silver on the bleached wood posts — sticks, really — that held up the fence's wires. I stood near the fence and listened, caught up in a silence so complete it seemed only the movement of the sun could properly register time's passing. Nothing sounded but the wind. A half-mile away a silent truck moved through a cloud of slow-rising dust. Then there was nothing.

I walked up to the fence and pulled out a small stick tied to a piece of barbed wire. It had been jammed between the fence and the endpost of the fencegate in such a way that it held the end-post up rigid. With the stick removed and the gate's endpost out of its shallow hole, the fencegate fell over, and I stepped over it into the cemetery.

Hammered into the grey dirt among the bunchgrass were old white-painted wooden crosses — the names and dates handwrit-ten on them. I saw no monuments of granite or marble.

But among the crosses stood a new, heavier, varnished cross. It widened out at the bottom and had a thunderbird head on top painted in blue and red. A little totem. This grave was fresh: a piece of yellow ribbon, a red ribbon, some bouquets, and two overturned plastic vases containing dried-up flowers lay scat-tered about on it, blown by the wind.

I stared at the grave. Garish, loud in its shapes and colours, it seemed completely different from what was around it. The simple white crosses were poetic: they evoked time and legend, old cowboy and Indian stories that carried the pathos of the past. Look at those crosses and you were reconciled to everything — whatever agony had occurred here had been transformed into objects that seemed as much as the bunchgrass to bend to the wind and partake of the desert silence.

But this new grave cut through all that. With its squat thunderbird head, its messy flowers and already-faded ribbons, it shouted with the pain of present-day life. I looked at the blown-about things and thought: An actual family has been here. Grief and politics had mixed, were inseparable. What I saw seemed poignant, an attempt to break a kind of spell and do something new. The very garishness of the blue and red thunderbird head and plastic vases of flowers seemed to express contorted, red-faced unhappiness in all its shaming force. Anger was here, and its presence bestowed a life-giving impurity.

The grave existed in the context of modern life: beyond the graveyard I could see two satellite dishes (so science-fiction-like there in the desert) and the reserve's new, vinyl-sided houses spaced far apart with no trees around them. But the grave also existed in the context of nature — the wind, the heat, the brilliant sun, the mesa west of the plateau that rose up dark and mythical in the late afternoon light. I felt the complexity of what was around me; and just as I had looking in the store window on Granville Street, but in a new way, I was mentally quickened.

The Third Floor

1

One day over thirty years ago I was sitting in the Vancouver Public Library reading a book of poems. Another man sat at the table, a man of about forty. His eyes caught mine.

"Look at this."

I looked over. He was staring at me and moving one of his hands. It took me a few moments to understand what was going on, but then I realized that he had his cock – half-erect, still bent over — out of his pants.

I said, "Excuse me," and got up. I got my book and walked away to another floor.

The book was by John Newlove, the Canadian poet. He had a poem about lonely men that I read over and over:

> It is a man

> It sits in the public library
> coveting the women it fears.

> They sense it has been without a woman for a long
>   time
> and they loathe it.

They smell the worst kind of celibacy on it,
involuntary.

When I read these lines I thought: That's me. I could see
myself in Newlove's man. I was like him. When Alistair and I
went into the Egmont or the Anchor on a weekday afternoon,
we'd push up the sleeves on our V-neck sweaters and hold our
glasses of beer with our left hands even when the glasses were
on the terrycloth table. We'd drink, but we had nothing to say to
each other. We were young, trying hard to be men, and the men
we imitated didn't talk.

2

Cate had left me. I'd moved out of the basement suite we'd shared
for a year and gotten myself the small one-room apartment mentioned in my essay on Michel Tremblay.

That first day I had a hard time opening the window. When it
finally jerked up on its cords and the cool air blew in, I stuck my
head out. I could see a huge puddle on the flat tarpaper roof of
the glass factory across the alley. It reflected the late afternoon
sky, clearing up now after the day's rain.

How alive those blue and violet colours seemed! I was still
young enough that I lived in a world where everything resembled something else, and now I shivered. In those long streaks
of colour in the puddle and in the white and black clouds that
floated above them I saw Cate as a vision of kindness leaning out
of the sky and smiling at me.

When I'd lived with her we'd gone to the library at least once
a week. Our library cards were made of paper. The books had
manila envelopes pasted into them for the date-stamp cards. The
librarians liked us; Cate and I gossiped about them afterward.

"Do you think she has a boyfriend?" Cate said.

"I doubt it."

"But people have secrets."

"Do you have secrets?" I said.

"Yes I have secrets." She smiled. "Don't you?"

"Oh yeah."

She liked getting me books. My favourite of the writers she introduced me to was Solzhenitsyn. I loved the scene at the end of *Cancer Ward* where Oleg goes out to buy clothes and the clerk asks him for the neck *and* sleeve size of his shirt, and Oleg feels embarrassed at the clerk's decadence. Tremendous, I thought. That's the way to act. They were great, dry, virile books, those Solzhenitsyn novels.

When Cate left, the books I'd read when she was still with me became suffused with an aura. I reread them for that aura, just as I went to Stanley Park to feel her presence. It'd been our habit to walk around Lost Lagoon, then go through the underpass and over to where the kids played on the swings. We'd sit on the grass on a blanket and talk about what the kids were doing.

"See, that little boy is *angry*," Cate said. "He doesn't want to swing, but he doesn't want her to swing either."

"How d'you know that."

"Oh, I just know."

She sat smiling with her legs under her like a child herself, except that her bare thighs showed below her minidress and I wanted, as I did every day I knew her, to push that skirt up yet again and lie on top of her.

Now I lay on my back on the grass near where the kids played. I watched them or stared at the sky. The hours passed. It seemed like a sickness, what I felt, and it seemed I would never get over it.

3

A would-be writer lived in the attic above me. His name was Albert McIntyre and over time he introduced me to a wider world.

Albert was skinny and sarcastic, with long black hair and high cheekbones that made me think he was Indian. In the summer he walked around Vancouver in jeans and runners with just a vest over his bare chest. Young women liked him. One night when we were drinking in the Biltmore on Kingsway a pretty but rough-looking girl came through the crowd and sat down with us. She wore a miniskirt and thigh-high boots: Albert had been signalling her. Now he began to talk to her, banter with her, coming down hard on his consonants so that everything he said had a tough, Northwest Territories edge.

"I got a gun," he said. "I want to shoot you with my gun. You want to get murdered?"

She shrugged and pushed a hand through her hair and her skirt moved up higher on her thigh. "Sure — I'd like to get murdered."

My heart pounded. I thought: So that's how you do it.

4

Albert and I had run into each other at a house in Kitsilano where once a month a government-funded writers' group got together. There were a couple of girls at these get-togethers who frightened me though I could hardly stay away from them. One night I read a Donald Barthelme-style story about a young man unbuttoning the navy blue skirt of a young woman and talking to her in a coolly ironic way while he did it, and her responding but then finally stopping him at the last minute because, after all, conventions count.

"That's *good*," one of the girls said. "You got any more stories like that?"

"Oh yeah," I said. But I didn't.

Because of that story Albert wanted to get to know me more. But first we had to drink. That was how I met his mentor. Albert knew an older man, a Ukrainian-Canadian who'd had his stories read on CBC radio. This Ukrainian and four or five other writers would drink beer at the Austin, and the Ukrainian would tell them the way things were. He loved the South American surrealists and German books like *Soul of Wood*.

That first night he said to me: "Serafin. So you're Polish. You know anything about the Second World War?"

I looked at him: beard like a spade, thin cheeks, hard little suffering eyes under overhanging eyebrows. He looked like a Bolshevik.

"Sure," I said. "I know a bit."

"Do you know that the Ukrainians were systematically murdered and slaughtered by the Poles? They were butchered — and they were butchers."

He laughed — then opened his arms wide and dropped his head in an exaggerated apologetic shrug. He was drunk.

"Forgive me. You look European. Listen to Bartok, my friend Bruce. All the horror is there."

About a week later I ran into Albert in the library.

He pointed to my book, getting the jump on me. "What you got there?"

I showed him: *The Beastly Beatitudes of Balthazar B.*

"Lightweight. Read *The Mulatta and Mister Fly.* There's semen in Asturias. Cock and cunt. Listen. I got a poem for you," Albert said, and we sat down at one of the tables. Albert read in his theatrically aggressive voice, which I now recognized derived from the Ukrainian, bearing down hard on the consonants as if he was striking fire from a piece of flint:

> Red night!
> The stunned hunger in cars —

The librarian glanced our way, quietly shushed us. Albert's voice turned into a hissing whisper full of *t*s and *s*s.

When he finished, images filled the room as if the city had poured out of his mouth.

"That's great, man," I said. I felt sick with jealousy.

"What're you writing?"

I shook my head. "Nothing. Nothing."

On a rainy morning not long after, I sat in the library staring at a book by Osip Mandelstam. For no reason I began to weep. For months now I'd eaten only doughnuts, take-out eggrolls and porridge, coffee and beer, and though I didn't know it I was sick. I weighed about 120 pounds. I was wearing a parka over an old sweater and not only was I crying, I was sweating and shivering at the same time and felt like I was going to faint any second.

The librarian came over and touched my shoulder.

"Are you all right?"

I put my hand to my eyebrows, like somebody shielding their eyes. I stared at my book. It was so good to have somebody care for me! I felt like bawling. But I was a man.

"I'm okay. I'm all right."

"Well, if you need any help just let me know. All right?"

"Sure," I said, still staring at the book. I wanted to wipe my eyes. But already I felt better.

5

I had another friend named Tim Clermont. He was big and very tall, with a long face and bristly hair and hot dark eyes behind granny glasses. Tim was a draft dodger from Baltimore who was fuelled by an enormous anxiety that he kept as much under wraps as he could. I'd met him at Langara College, where I'd gone for a few months and ended up doing little besides listen to Rimsky-Korsakov's "Scheherezade" in the music room and watch the snow fall on the stucco houses of South Vancouver.

Booktalk was Tim's release. On the bus one day, he became so worked up about writers that I became embarrassed. The louder he talked the softer I talked. Finally we got to where I was nearly whispering.

"You can't compare Eugenio Montale to *any* American poets!" Tim shouted, oblivious to the looks he was getting for saying the word "poets" out loud on a bus.

"You're probably right," I muttered.

"Even the brilliance of *detail* in Montale —"

"I know what you mean —"

"You don't know what I mean! What do you mean, you know what I mean!"

"I just mean that I know Montale's a good writer."

"Oh for fuck sakes. 'A good writer.'" Tim shook his head and looked out the window, bitterly angry.

Then one day Albert read to us from a play he'd started about his childhood in Ontario.

His attic room was dark, lamplit — there was no window. A mattress lay on the floor; a fridge hummed; a rickety card table with a typewriter on it shook each time it was touched; folding chairs stood around it; and on one shadowed wall *Penthouse* foldouts gleamed — open-mouthed women showing their pubic hair, their stockinged legs spread wide there in the dark.

Tim detested the foldouts. He hadn't wanted to come. But I'd dragged him along because I was obsessed with Albert and I wanted Tim to share that obsession. I wanted a gang — I wanted the three of us to mix our power.

And now Albert was reading with his head down, his hand gesturing slightly. Tim's cheeks reddened and he put his arms around himself, one across his chest and one diagonally up to his shoulder.

The play — or part-play: Albert read for about twenty minutes — took place in a trailer and involved a terrified boy trying to escape the cruelties of his parents. It overwhelmed me. I thought I had never heard anything finer. When Albert finished he jerked his head up at me. "What do you think?"

The question was uncharacteristic.

"Oh it's good. Yeah, it's really good."

Tim said nothing. We both looked at him. His face was red. He didn't move a muscle.

I felt an immediate anger. "Well, say something man."

"Mucus. Shit. Bloody piss. Glass in the throat."

The fridge hummed. Tim got up and went out, walking as fast as he could, almost running down the stairs.

I looked at Albert. A few seconds later I went after Tim. Out on the street I ran up to him and touched his shoulder.

"Hey Tim. Wait up."

He kept walking. I walked beside him.

"Are you okay?" I gave him a quick look.

He whispered, "Sure. I'm fine."

Then: "It's all just such bullshit ... I don't know what I'm doing ... I don't know, you know? You know? ... I just feel bad. I just had to get out of there."

He looked at me. "Thanks for coming after me."

I shook my head slightly. "No problem." After we had walked for a bit, I said, "I had nothing better to do."

6

And one winter night I met Cate in the library. It was something I'd dreamt of again and again: I'd be in the Egmont, drunk, and I'd imagine her coming in the door and walking through the crowd in her yellow sweater and tight white jeans over to where I sat; or I'd be coming home down Broadway and I'd imagine that when I went up the stairs and opened the brown door to my room, she'd be there, sitting with her legs under her on my bed waiting for me.

Now here she was. My heart jumped in my chest at the shock. Under her long coat she was wearing jeans and a red and black checked blouse that I remembered. Her hair was in her eyes.

"Hi," she said.

"Hi," I said.

"How are you doing?"

"I'm doing fine."

I glared at her and turned away. How I wanted to hurt her! I went down one of the rows of books. Turning my head sideways, I looked at the spines of the books without seeing them. My heart pounded. Finally I straightened up and looked back.

She was gone.

And now my stomach lurched with unhappiness and panic. I went looking for her. I searched the third floor, the second. On the mezzanine I said to one of the librarians, "Have you seen a girl in a long brown coat come by in the last few minutes?"

She hadn't.

I went down to the main floor and searched it. Then I went outside and ran up and down Robson in the dark and the cold. She was gone.

Finally I went back in. I was shivering. I sat at a table and blinked my eyes. Then after a while I got up and went up the stairwell to the third floor where my coat was. I put it on and began searching, going through the stacks, reading titles, picking out book after book until I had a pile in my arms that made me feel protected and assuaged.

Those days are gone now. Fewer and fewer things bring them to mind – some books, some back streets. The library itself is gone. Even the faces on the buses look different. They have become a myth, a legend, less. And there's no sense being upset about it. But I teach, now, after all – substantive editing at Douglas College in New Westminster – and sometimes when I look at my students laughing or making faces at each other, I think of telling them about some people I knew who were their age who evoked everything that literature meant to me when I was young.

Dead on the Shelf

1

When I was fifteen my friend Alistair and I would take the bus over to the book store in Park Royal. On the very bottom shelf, below even Yevgeny Yevtushenko's *Babi Yar and Other Poems* and Carl Sandberg's *Honey and Salt* lay copies of the literary magazine *Talon*. It was published in North Vancouver. Each issue cost thirty cents. Sitting in the mall drinking an Orange Julius and eating a hot dog we'd read our copies from front to back.

Fed by the time and place we lived in, the poems in *Talon*, written sometimes by kids still in high school, gave us news about beauty and the management of words. Reading them, we received, without consciously knowing it, our deepest understanding about art: it has to be new. However trembling or amateurish, however awkward, art lives by its newness. We saw this, the basic fact about art (so often buried later by bad education), as all adolescents do, and it thrilled us. Because they contained the new, those poems in *Talon* mattered to us at least as much as the amazing poems by Ginsberg and Ferlinghetti and McClure that we read and re-read in *The New American Poetry: 1945–1960*.

In front of me now lie copies of a bunch of BC's current literary journals: *Prism International, Malahat Review, Event, West Coast Line, Capilano Review, Writing, Geist,* and *subTerrain*. It's hard, going through them, to remember all that I felt when Alistair and I, eating our hot dogs, would read our copies of *Talon*, lingering over each page. But before I get to that, a word about the magazines. If you're familiar with these journals you know that they fall into two groups: the university mags, which are supported by an educational institution and subsidized by both the provincial and federal governments; and the two city magazines, as I'll call them, *Geist* and *subTerrain*, which are independent.

The university mags — *Writing, Capilano Review, Event, Prism International, West Coast Line* and *Malahat Review* — are all more or less the same: paperback book format (glued binding, roughly 6 x 9 inches, 100 or so pages), austere page design, heavily subsidized, supported by an institution, overwhelmingly devoted to the conventional literary poem and short story. *Sub-TERRAIN* is more like *Geist*: it's supported by ads, sales, and a casino, it has a magazine format, and while it does print mostly stories and poems, it seems more urban and punchy than the subsidized university magazines — a quality you especially notice in its bold layout.

2

I've spent the past few weeks looking at two or three issues of each of these journals. Now I've arrived at some conclusions.

In the first place, with the exception of *subTerrain* and *Geist*, all of these magazines look the same. They all have the same paperback book format, the same austere table of contents and interior design, the same horror of any sort of pizzazz in their layout. To look at an issue of *Event* or *Prism* or any of the other magazines is to look at a journal that to an astounding degree refuses to catch your attention. Wraps, cover text, ads, heads and decks, an evocative table of contents, a bold layout that delights your eye if you happen to flip through the mag – you find none of this. One might argue that the university journals are sold more by subscription than on the newsstands, and so don't have to worry so much about being picked out from a sea of brilliantly designed products. But this argument doesn't stand up. After all, magazines such as *Granta* and the *New York Review of Books*, to name just two out of many, are also sold mostly by subscription, and they are both superbly designed. What's the difference? The difference is that these magazines are out to *gain* readers and *keep* them, and they know that to do these things an attractive – and, if I might say so, alive — package matters.

But look at our university journals. You just have to open them to see how little they feel the need to appeal to an audience. What stirs and motivates *their* editors isn't so much gaining an audience as it is realizing a platonic ideal of what a little magazine should be — an ideal which in the case of the journals being looked at here is almost absurdly out of date. Between Harriett Monroe's *Poetry*, which first appeared in 1912, and *West Coast Line* or *Writing* or the *Malahat Review*, there hardly exists any difference in format.

What amazes me here is that an enormous amount of thought has gone into magazine design since 1912, all of it in an attempt to attract and sustain readers' attention. The result can be seen in the wonderfully designed periodicals that are on the stands today, from *La Lettre* to *True Crime*. In comparison to these, our own literary magazines look painfully timid, locked into a provincial ideal of "elegance" and "the clean page" that could only exist in an environment in which the audience doesn't matter.

But put format aside. The content of these magazines also reflects their lack of interest in gaining and sustaining an audience. Again with the exception of *Geist* and *subTerrain*, the journals being looked at here are overwhelmingly precious. What a stifling belles-lettrism, what a smell of the creative writing class and the Vancouver poetry circle rises from the pages of these journals! They contain no photographs apart from the most pretentious "art photography," no vivid graphics, no comic strips, no journalistic articles, no intellectual polemics, no gossip, no humour, no genre fiction (crime stories, science-fiction stories, *Redbook*-style romances), no columns, almost no editorial notes, no political opinion, in some cases no reviews of any sort, no sense of place (the university magazines are not noticeably "rooted" in any specific city or town) and above all none of the sense of topicality, of being something that comes out on a historical timeline, that makes us turn to magazines instead of books in the first place. Instead these magazines offer precisely the two literary genres that are the most disliked by the print-reading audience: the poem and the sensitive short story. These are both genres in which unless the piece is *exceptionally* vigorous, it will go unread; yet page after page of the *Capilano Review* and *West Coast Line* and the rest of them are filled with just such unread stuff to the exclusion of anything else.

The result? Well, whenever I talk to the serious readers I know about whether or not they look at BC's little magazines, I get the same response. "Are you kidding? Maybe, *maybe*, if I have a piece of my own in one of the issues, I'll flip through it; otherwise, I'd rather have a tooth pulled than read a copy of *Prism* or any of the rest of those rags."

Significant here is what my printhound acquaintances *do* read on those rare occasions when they turn to these magazines. They read the contributors' notes; they read the editorial note, if there is one; if the book reviews are short and punchy enough, they read the reviews. In other words, they read everything that escapes the precious garden of sensitive writing and ties the magazine, in however slight a way, to the big world.

But it isn't just that. My acquaintances also read what they can scan, what they can take in at a glance, which of course is exactly what we all do when we first pick up a magazine. One of the most important things influencing magazine design these days is the recognition that modern readers always perform a *two-step* reading when they go through a journal. There's a first scan, where we read heads, decks, callouts, photos, short fragments of text, whatever catches our eye and can be more or less immediately taken in; and then there's a second and more traditional reading, where we go from paragraph to paragraph as we do when we read a book. A journal that refuses to allow for this two-step reading doesn't just bore us. It presents itself as impenetrable, which is precisely the case with six of the eight magazines being looked at here. They starve the reader when he or she first goes through them, presenting themselves as mags that have "nothing in them." As a result, they are almost invariably put down unread after they have been flipped through.

3

Why are our little magazines like this?

Let's consider the fact that the six most boring journals being discussed here are also the ones entirely dependent on both the academy and the government for their existence. This fact matters. It isn't philistine to ask why these magazines have taxpayer-subsidized budgets of thousands of dollars per issue, yet put out minuscule print runs of which only a quarter or even less are read. When I and some friends decided to start the *Vancouver Review* in 1990, one of the things that most motivated us was our irritation at the so often thoughtless complicity between the government funding agencies and the magazines that they subsidized. If you published reviews and journalism and distributed your magazine free in order to get it to a large audience, you couldn't (and still can't) receive funding from the Canada Council, no matter how interesting and widely-read your reviews and journalism were.

It was, and is, madness: initiative wasn't rewarded, an attempt to connect with an audience wasn't rewarded; and when we sat around and thought about what our magazine should do, one of the things we most wanted was to have the magazine state this in a way that couldn't be ignored. (In particular we wanted to point out that the utter blandness and provinciality of the criticism the journals produced was due precisely to their cosseted situation.)

The frustrating fact of the matter both then and now is that magazines like *West Coast Line* or *The Malahat* or *Event* or *Prism* simply don't need to be concerned about gaining an audience. These magazines won't fold if only a hundred people read them. They won't fold if only twenty people read them. And because they have no real need for readers, they are strikingly, almost bewilderingly boring.

4

But the deepest problem with these journals isn't that they're subsidized. They wouldn't be worth writing about if that was all that was wrong with them. What matters much more is their effect on BC's writers and their lack of impact in BC itself.

Ever since William Wordsworth wrote his "Preface" to the *Lyrical Ballads* at the beginning of the nineteenth century, what might be called high literary art, and in particular, poetry, has moved away from the social arena — the arena of Shakespeare and Ben Jonson and Swift and Pope. It has moved away from the culture of cities and indeed from popular culture in general, and cultivated instead a realm in which the private sensibility has an overwhelming importance. Wordsworth pointed with contempt and disgust to

> the increasing accumulation of men in cities, where the uniformity of their occupations produces a craving for extraordinary incident, which the rapid communication of intelligence hourly gratifies. To this tendency of life and manners the literature and theatrical exhibitions of the country have conformed themselves. The invaluable works of our elder writers ... are driven into neglect by frantic novels, sickly and stupid German tragedies, and deluges of idle and extravagant stories in verse.

Against this growing influence of melodramatic writing, with its suspense and pathos — which is to say, the growing influence of the novel, above all — Wordsworth proposed a "philosophic" literature: "its object is truth, not individual and local, but general and operative, not standing upon external testimony, but carried alive into the heart by passion"; and from 1805 until now this has been the determining principle of high literary art.

And why does this matter? It matters because here in BC, as in other peripheral societies, this "high culture," dominated by the government and the universities, and lacking a marketplace in which new ideas can circulate, is all we have. Our popular culture, our vital culture, comes from elsewhere.

In particular it comes from the US. Who reading this won't admit that they've spent far more time with *Harper's* or the *New Yorker*, or even, say, *Grand Street* or *Sulfur*, than they've spent reading all of Canada's literary and cultural magazines put together? Who hasn't been influenced by American journals? Who hasn't had their thinking, their way of engaging the world, fundamentally shaped by them?

We live in a colonial country and an even more colonial province. For exactly that reason magazines could be a great vehicle for BC's writers, more so even than books, since in the early 21st century, with our intense awareness of history, our deep sense of being caught up in time, the periodical, which comes out on a timeline, satisfies a fundamental desire to see ourselves reflected from week to week and month to month. We are all magazine readers, even if we rarely read novels or stories. Little magazines could be a place for us to learn to write a new kind of poetry that people want to read. We could learn how to write essays and cartoon strips, how to take pictures, how to talk about our frontier cultures, our cities, our bowling alleys, our sidewalks and fantasies and political issues, and so enter the cultural arena in a new and vital way.

But as long as our magazines continue to present themselves as captive to a pale, institutional dream this won't happen. The idea that art is what is new will become lost. And this, finally, is the worst thing about BC's little magazines as they now stand. Read by young writers, they inevitably encourage young writers to produce precisely the kind of work that they themselves print: academically sanctioned work no one wants to read. Ultimately they leave BC's writers even more on the sidelines of the big culture than they already are, with poems in *West Coast Line* or *Event* or the *Malahat Review*, maybe, but ultimately outside of the real cultural arena, reading other men's and women's strong books, reading other magazines, fantasizing about everywhere except where they in fact are.

Avant-Garde
Mentalitites

1

Here are two quotations. I invite you to look at them as much for their vocabulary and syntax as for their content:

1. The reader enters the text as an under-determined code and fixes certain reading paths as *favored*. In "Codicil" the expression is composed almost entirely of isolated, non-integrating lexemes that a reader can infer as referring only to a lexicon, i.e., to the most basic properties of the units of meaning involved. From this basic dictionary code a number of readings can be built. A reader might progress to an operation of establishing textual differences, similarities, acoustic pattern or contrast, discontinuities in sense/sound etc. Productional inferences may also be made by resorting to intertextual frames and the text will be read within the interventional and modificational factors of the empirical reader's experience of *other* texts.

2. Whereby we see that in the total system of the image the structural functions are polarized; on the one hand there is a sort of paradigmatic condensation on the level of connotators (i.e., by and large, of the "symbols"), which are strong, erratic, and one might say "reified" signs; and on the other there is a syntagmatic "flow" on the level of

denotation; it will not be forgotten that the syntagm is always very close to speech, and it is indeed the iconic "discourse" which naturalizes its symbols.

One of these quotations comes from Steve McCaffery's book *North of Intention*. One comes from an essay written in the sixties by Roland Barthes. Can you tell them apart? If you're familiar with Barthes's work you probably can. But even if you're not, just on the strength of these passages I think you can see that McCaffery writes very much like the structuralist Barthes. He has the same density, the same quasi-scientific vocabulary, the same coolly objective viewpoint, the same commitment to a kind of exhaustive exploration of the text being considered, and the same dependence on the idea that a piece of writing is first and foremost a linguistic structure whose effect is determined by the laws of language.

This influential style originated in France in the early sixties. It has had a tremendous impact on avant-garde criticism in Canada. Its difference from conventional criticism written in English — above all, its verbal density — makes it very attractive to some writers. In Vancouver, McCaffery's use of this style has turned him into a bit of a cult figure. Those who admire him admire his assimilation of French thought and his ability to use this thought to describe the writing of marginal or avant-garde writers in Canada and the US; for them, reading McCaffery is a little like having a brilliant French critic right here at home.

Well, I like Barthes, too, very much. And to some extent I'm sympathetic with the viewpoint of McCaffery's fans. Yet it seems to me that another way to look at his work is more revealing. And that is to see it as colonial — as work that mimics a body of "master texts" originating elsewhere. Seen in this way, McCaffery resembles those early Canadian poets who wrote in the style of Swinburne or Tennyson; as with them, the chief thing you notice in his work is an unconscious pathos, the pathos of whatever is derivative or second-hand without meaning to be so. Each time I opened *North of Intention*, sometimes to read an essay, sometimes just to drift, noting a phrase here, a word there, I realized I had seen many of those words and phrases elsewhere; I noticed McCaffery's infatuation with the more superficial stylistic aspects of French criticism, and his consequent inability to *steal* from the writers he uses and so make their ideas his own. Indeed, his mimicry of the French style was so blatant that I felt the only thing notable about the book was its epigonism: in the end the real interest of *North of Intention* seemed to me to lie in the fact that it was the work of a writer who was like other writers, a characteristic figure.

2

To start with, McCaffery has a strongly collegial sensibility — something he shares with many members of the Vancouver avant-garde, such as the members of the Kootenay School of Writing (who have as their their website motto: "We Will Not Be Understood," a rather elegant play on an old Vancouver department store slogan). Like an astronaut, or a tenured sociologist, he is a colleague, someone involved in a project that he develops in a "responsible" manner for others who are similarly involved. His writing is determined and given shape by an extremely strong sense of solidarity: as with the sixties Barthes, he writes for a group, a group to which he is wedded, right down to the style of his prose.

For Barthes, this group was the structuralists and avant-garde writers who produced work for the magazines *Communications* and *Tel Quel*; and for McCaffery it is the "language-centered" writers clustered around the magazines $L=A=N=G=U=A=G=E$ and *Open Letter*. He writes for them, it's from them that he gets his sense of what is worth doing; and in each of his sentences, and even his choice of words, an emphatic need for solidarity with the group can be felt.

Another characteristic quality I will call McCaffery's heroism. This heroism is due in part to the verbal density — the atmosphere of difficulty — that McCaffery has borrowed from the French; but it is due even more to the lofty, impersonal tone that his solidarity with the group gives him. It is the tone of someone whose very language is determined by the collective that gives him its strength, and it can occasionally lead to absurdity.

One of the pieces collected in *North of Intention*, for instance, is an interview with McCaffery conducted by Andrew Payne. At one point, after discussing the avant-garde writers who are McCaffery's subjects, Payne asks the following:

> *Andy*: I wonder if we don't find, in a lot of this work, a kind of mono-dimensionality of "tone" . . . at times, too, a lack of humor.
>
> *Steve*: Yes, Creeley mentioned this in a recent issue of *Sagetrieb*, although I'm not sure of the validity of any generalization here. I've personally come to see humor as a useful tonal-ideological destabilizer, an agent of relativization, dispersal and inversion (similar to Bakhtin's notion of the carnivalization of literature). Humor tends to operate as a visceral, or tactile investment upon the level of the verbal order; it is not entirely "of" language.

This is practically self-parody; but what really interests me here is the stolidity of McCaffery's response, the unblinking assurance, the complete reliance on a kind of "secured" vocabulary. Here you see the house style not only of the avant-garde, but of any large government corporation, a style whose chief purpose is to mask the individual writer and give him a kind of group sensibility.

At bottom, it is an unfree style. In prose, at least, you get across the sense of a freely speaking voice by using dramatic arrhythmia — digressions, questions, changes in register, the interruption of a mass of complex sentences with a short declarative one. But almost none of this linguistic drama appears in McCaffery. Instead he uses a colleague's sentence — long, impersonal, jargon-ridden — that imposes its rhythm on the work to the exclusion of any other. This effectively masks McCaffery as an individual, while making him stand out as a heroic representative of a project and program of work.

McCaffery's methodology is also characteristic. It consists

of a kind of exhaustive "covering" of the text being considered in which you bring to bear every piece of knowledge you have that might be relevant or in some sense illuminating. This is the structuralist approach (Barthes said that all he could do as a structuralist was "cover" the texts he dealt with), but it also comes close to what in English is called *bullshitting*. The difference between the two is largely a matter of tact and of having a sense of proportion, but it is exactly these qualities that are missing from much of McCaffery's work. Consider the following extract from an article on George Bowering's *Allophanes*:

> *Allophanes* ... emerges beneath two signatories, two proprietors: the author (George Bowering), whose proper name will authenticate the book, and a dictator, Jack Spicer, a disembodied voice, whose proper name reformulates the deceased, primal father of Freud's *Totem and Taboo* and who, as a spectral subject, haunts the text's temporal unwindings to a degree that can never be fully ascertained.
>
> Pretending to be inaugural, the sign could only endlessly mime its own circularity, since it has already constituted to designate — to whom? — its own birth. Mythology imprisons this tautological figure into that of a Monster, a Sphere, an Egg where the nothingness unites with Being, and whose multiple names — Noun, Kneph, Okeanos, Ouroboros, Aion, Leviathan, Ain-Soph, etc. — arbitrarily conjure up that which *in principle* has no appelation, as though to deny to thought the access to its own silence.

The essay goes on like this for pages. Like those student papers that bring masses of Kierkegaard and Hegel to bear on a novel by Kurt Vonnegut, say, and so end up sounding intensely sophomoric, McCaffery has brought a huge load of knowledge to bear on Bowering's little book, without at any point demonstrating that the book can handle it.

3

Most of the essays in *North of Intention* deal with avant-garde poets, especially McCaffery's colleagues in what has come to be known as the language school of poetry. I offer here the opening sentences of three of these essays:

1. We will focus on the ludic features of *The Martyrology*, those varieties of wordplay (pun, homophony, palindrome, anagram, paragram, charade), which relate writing to the limits of intentionality and the Subject's own relation to meaning.

2. This essay investigates a single aspect of Bissett's work: the aspect of excess and libidinal flow, of the interplay of forces and intensities, both through and yet quite frequently despite, language; the flow of non-verbal energies through verbal domains that registers most often as a sheer libidinal will to power, a schizop(oetic)hrenic strategy to break through the constraint mechanisms of grammar and classical discourse in general.

3. We can trace in Jackson Mac Low's work the putting into play of a kind of writing machine that opens up scriptive practice to an infinite semiosis through the infra-textual and combinatory nature of words.

You can see from these quotations that McCaffery tends to use the collegial "we," that his tone is coolly objective, and that he is interested above all in exploring the linguistic practices of his writers — in short, that he functions as a student or academic. And this would be fine. The trouble here is that McCaffery is bringing a scholarly type of criticism to bear on writers whose interest lies chiefly in their eccentricity. By "scholarly" I mean the kind of work usually found in academic articles on Kafka or Blake or William Congreve — i.e., articles that take the literary worth of their authors for granted and subject them to little or no evaluation, being interested instead in some aspect of what they have done.

Now by treating his writers this way McCaffery is making a claim about them: he is implying that their literary worth is in some sense indisputable. And again, this is characteristic. Throughout the literary avant-garde you find enormous claims being made for writers that the common reader finds tedious or unintelligible — the treatment of bp Nichol is a great example of this — and you find these claims being made in the context of the academy, where reader interest doesn't count. In short, like a number of his peers, McCaffery wants to legitimate his colleagues, to stake a claim for them by discussing them in the kind of cool non-judgemental way that Keats or Jane Austen might be discussed.

There are real difficulties with this approach. First, it leads to a fatuity or "deadness" which is hard to describe, though it is easy enough to sense when you come across it. What causes it? Mainly, I think, a lack of any sense of proportion on the part of the critic. I have already pointed out how this lack distorts McCaffery's article on *Allophanes* — an article in which he makes Bowering's book seem "major" by dumping a great mass of knowledge onto the work, regardless of whether it can bear it or not. But the other side of this approach should also be considered, since it amounts to a kind of conspiracy of silence. If bp Nichol is a major poet, for instance, and is treated as such, then what do you do with someone like Czeslaw Milosz? Why, you ignore him, in order not to give the game away.

Both these devices or methods of approach appear everywhere in avant-garde criticism. Add to them a fake or superficial objectivity, an often quite staggering pomposity in the choice of vocabulary and sentence structure, and a "seriousness" which is self-serving and tends to take the place of a strongly aesthetic sensibility, and you have the chief qualities that contribute to the air of fatuity that characterizes the kind of criticism McCaffery writes.

But there is a deeper problem. Such criticism really doesn't serve the writers it aims to legitimate. A lot could be said about the language poets, for instance, especially about their relationship to mass media such as radio and TV; but it simply won't *get* said unless a genuine tension exists between the critic and the writer being discussed.

But look at McCaffery's book. Not one of the essays collected here *questions* the text being considered, or even subjects it to the shock of skepticism. (There are no genuinely pointed asides in the entire volume). Instead McCaffery is in a sort of complicity with his writers: either he treats their work in exactly the way the writers would like it to be treated, or else he assumes that the literary and linguistic intentions of the critic and of the writer being discussed are the same. So that you learn from *North of Intention* not what the writers being discussed are like. You learn the right attitude to take to them.

I am being harsh. Plainly, McCaffery intends a kind of heroic defence of the writers he talks about. (bp Nichol, Fred Wah, bill bissett, George Bowering, and Christopher Dewdney are just a few of the poets who are either discussed or quoted in *North of Intention*.) Some of these writers are more interesting than others, some are barely readable; but taken together they constitute a core sample of the literary avant-garde — the "zoo of the new," to use Sylvia Plath's phrase.

Now this is an interesting zoo, and I imagine most readers of literature would want to hear about it. Yet to deal with it properly requires qualities that are implicit in Plath's phrase. Youthful qualities: brightness, vivacity, curiosity, and above all the kind of quick-eyed temperament that can both *see* and clearly evoke the exotic animals before it.

But none of these qualities appears in McCaffery's book. And this is because the true object of his attention isn't the avant-garde zoo, but the great mass of European writers in whose shadow he and his colleagues huddle. The writers who matter in this book are European. They include Roland Barthes, Roman Jakobson, Julia Kristeva, Gilles Deleuze, Jean Baudrillard, Jacques Derrida, and Mikhail Bakhtin, and what sticks out as their names tumble forth is how passive McCaffery is in the face of their authority.

Two consequences follow. First, the influence of these writers
has led McCaffery to all but forsake the particular genius of his
own language; it has led him, that is, to write a prose that doesn't
just lump together the ideas of these writers, but also pastiches
their styles. And so (the second consequence) his work drones. It
has that dull sameness of tone that invariably speaks of timidity
or, more exactly, of a writer's boredom with what he is producing. Because he has forsaken his Native speech rhythms, and
in general the speed and elan of modern English, McCaffery's
writing offers no pleasure. On the contrary: his prose is so derivative and so removed from the language he speaks that his essays
have a brontosaurian quality. You feel he is producing the work
by will-power alone.

4

We live in an international age, a time when regional and cultural
boundaries are becoming less and less meaningful. For many
writers this has led to a kind of split between them and the place
in which they live. It is their home, certainly, they speak its language, its politics affect them, its streets and buildings are intimately familiar; yet many if not most of its concerns seem somehow parochial and unreal. What does it mean to live in Vancouver, for instance, if you read books translated from the French
and the German, if your magazines come from New York, your
TV shows come from New York, your car comes from Japan,
and last year you took that trip to Italy you'd been planning?
What seems certain is that over time a "world sense" develops;
the life one lives seems merely background.

For a writer this makes the concept of an audience difficult.
Where is the audience? Is it the audience that knows the same
jingles you know? Or is it the audience that shares your ideas?

These questions are especially hard for intellectuals. Again
and again they find a gap between the discourse they hear
around them and the discourse they turn to in books to keep
them stimulated. For them, the temptation to give up on the
local or even national scene, and hence to give up on its language,

can be overwhelming — as overwhelming as the complementary temptation to join forces with a like-minded group.

So a paradox arises: seeking the *largest* language, the language that seems most international, most part of an over-arching intellectual project, the critic ends up writing for fewer and fewer people. Wanting to be significant, he first of all loses his "place," then his sense of proportion, his ease with his Native speech, and finally his pleasure in the use of words.

The loss of speech: one keeps coming back to that. The pathos in McCaffery's work is the pathos of baffled effort, of a voice muffled by a kind of plate glass of borrowed styles. His texts are as misshapen as they are because he has lost the writer's intense connection to his own language. And I believe that this is a function of writing for a group. Do that — write for a group — and you gain security. Your writing becomes protected: you no longer know the anxiety of writing "blind," of wondering whether your work will be entertaining, or read. And without that anxiety the work turns bad. Intensity drains away: your writing becomes tedious, right-minded. You go to books for your ideas; you learn what you are supposed to say. Ultimately you become unfree.

Long Tall Sally

1

Remember the movie *Forrest Gump*, with Tom Hanks so good in the title role? Remember the sense — not so much of homesickness but of history sickness, historical nostalgia — that came over you as you watched the show? I know when I saw the movie I felt I shared in forty years of American experience. And I wasn't alone. All of us in the audience identified with the innocent fool Gump. And so it became possible for all of us to review together in an emotional way everything that had been tragic in American public life over the past four decades.

The fact that a Vancouver audience felt such a complete sense of sharing in American history shows the near-total effectiveness of the movie. It also demonstrates the amazing power of American popular culture, and (as I realized yet again a few years ago when I saw members of a Nelson, BC audience rise to its feet and clap at the end of *Air Force One*) it says something about our indifference to our own reality, a point I'll come back to later.

In a different way, in a different key, Don DeLillo's novel *Underworld* provides the same sensation of sharing in American life. *Forrest Gump* offered its weight of sorrow fully orchestrated, plush and obvious. *Underworld* gives its readers a keener, sharper melody. And along with the tensile strength of its sentences, the intricate structure of the book most contributes to its force.

The book opens with a 25,000 word Prologue, "The Triumph of Death," which many reviewers called a breakthough piece of prose for DeLillo. It first appeared in *Harper's* as the novella "Pafko at the Wall," and it describes the 1951 pennant race game between the New York Giants and the Brooklyn Dodgers, decided at the last minute by Bobby Thomson's "shot heard round the world." In the *New York Review of Books* Luc Sante suggested that the text

> is a tour de force of cinematic writing — not text that is camera-ready (as is practiced by too many writers these days), but that challenges the movies at their own game. It zooms, dollies, tracks, cuts from close-ups to long shots and back, assembles thousands of bits of visual and auditory information into a montage that spectacularly renders the entire experience. . . . He can not only deliver the effect of single shots spliced together ("A man slowly wiping his glasses. A staring man. A man flexing the stiffness out of his limbs") . . . he can also cut suddenly into and out of various viewpoints — four of them, though the effect is multitudinous.

The Prologue goes on for sixty pages, thrilling in its complexity, photographic in its precise, overlapping, black-and-white details, capturing everything — the whole ballgame and all that surrounds it. (The game the reader sees and hears even includes a brilliantly rendered conversation between J. Edgar Hoover, Jackie Gleason, Frank Sinatra and Toots Shor.) After the home run, the reader enters the mind of radio announcer Russ Hodges, one of the four viewpoints DeLillo has been moving in and out of:

> This is the thing that will pulse in his brain come old age and double vision and dizzy spells — the surge sensation, the leap of people already standing, that bolt of noise and joy when the ball went in. . . .
> The raincoat drunk is running the bases. They see him

round first, his hands paddling the air to keep him from
drifting into right field. He approaches second in a burst
of coattails and limbs and untied shoelaces and swinging
belt. They see he is going to slide and they stop and watch
him leave his feet. All the fragments of the afternoon collect around his airborne form. Shouts, batcracks, full blad-
ders and stray yawns, the sand-grain manyness of things
that can't be counted.

It is all falling indelibly into the past.

2

Then a cut. The Prologue ends and Part 1 — "Long Tall Sally:
Spring – Summer 1992" — begins. The protagonist, Nick Shay,
a taciturn man who works in waste management, is speaking: "I
was driving a Lexus through a rustling wind."

In that cut, in that movement between the two sentences
(physically separated, in this beautifully designed book, by a single page, black at the bottom) the deepest effect of *Underworld*
starts to be felt. As the book proceeds, the reader encounters
five more parts. Note how the chronology progresses: "Elegy
for Left Hand Alone: Mid-1980s – Early 1990s"; "The Cloud of
Unknowing: Spring 1978"; "Cocksucker Blues: Summer 1974";
"Better Things for Better Living Through Chemistry: Selected
Fragments Public and Private in the 1950s and 1960s"; and finally
"Arrangement in Gray and Black: Fall 1951 – Summer 1952."

In other words: the way this 827-page book is constructed
deliberately impedes our usual expectations when we read a
novel. It moves backwards in time, not forward. More precisely,
it doesn't move. It sits still. You move through it. *Underworld*
presents itself as a gigantic act of assemblage, a collage of pieces
that the reader travels through, instead of being carried along by.
As one thoughtful reviewer noted, you read *Underworld* somewhat the way you read Eliot's *The Wasteland*; to which I add that
as you read you *feel* the way you do when you read Eliot's poem.

How to describe this feeling? Obviously DeLillo could have

structured his book more conventionally. He could have gone straight from the ballgame to his dazzling evocation of the Italian Bronx in 1951 and then kept on going. But he took a risk because he wanted to produce a book that makes you feel the weight of history, the weight of memories. He wanted in the first place to evoke that ghostly, spread-out, sorrowful feeling — that often confused feeling which is nonetheless intense, as if you had dived to the bottommost stratum of experience — which you have when you wake from a dream in which the dead have come back, and 1969, say, or 1980 uneasily mixes with the present.

And in the second place he wanted to evoke that strange modern sense of history we've all developed from spending so much of our lives sitting in front of a TV set watching the news. Everything comes back on TV news, repeats itself: Tiananmen Square, last week's murder in White Rock, the end of World War One, an abduction in Saskatchewan ten years ago. Everything exists simultaneously.

And so it is in *Underworld*. As you read you develop a sense that the dozens of characters — the thousands of details — all have a simultaneous life. This odd simultaneity gives everything that happens in the book that modern historical quality of seeming to have always been there, to be recurring again and again. Maybe you've seen those black and white World War Two images that appear every so often on television — tanks moving through rubbled streets, Russian soldiers advancing on Berlin. Have you noticed how they never lose their power to convey the all-but-overwhelming weight of the 20th century? They keep reappearing. Hitler keeps reappearing. JFK keeps coming back. The helicopter gunships used in the Vietnam war — their particular shape and sound — again and again fill the TV screen. The young man standing in front of the tank in Tiananmen Square keeps returning.

It all keeps coming back. It is all there at once. A gigantic collage. Almost at the start of the twentieth century Eliot recognized that a new sensibility had developed in the West, a feeling that all of history was present at any given moment — that the dead kept returning, again and again. Moreover, he recognized that in connection with this strange new phenomenon the individual was no longer the significant factor. What counted was the crowd.

DeLillo concurs. "The future belongs to crowds," he wrote in *Mao II*. And in the third paragraph of *Underworld* he writes: "Longing on a large scale is what makes history."

In a recent interview DeLillo noted that he has been interested for years in the following passage in John Cheever's journals, written after Cheever attended a ballgame in Shea Stadium:

> The task of an American writer is not to describe the misgivings of a woman taken in adultery as she looks out of a window at the rain but to describe 400 people under the lights reaching for a foul ball ... or the faint thunder as 10,000 people, at the bottom of the eighth, head for the exits. The sense of moral judgements embodied in a migratory vastness.

A migratory vastness — no phrase I can think of better describes *Underworld*. And it explains in another way why DeLillo took the risk he did with this huge novel. Storytelling, with its forward-moving progression in time, always involves the fate of individuals, single selves. But history joins us to what is outside ourselves. It makes the self less important. (Which is why it was so crucial that Forrest Gump, if he was to embody recent American history, be an exemplary figure, almost a character out of a fairy tale.)

Does this seem too abstract? Actually it isn't hard to feel yourself as an historical being. Think of that eagerness you have to watch the evening news; and think of how you feel when you click it on, knowing that millions of others are doing the same thing. Think of how you feel when you watch a Nike ad, when you line up at London Drugs, when you stand still with others in an elevator, when you see the crowd you are part of reflected in the plate glass of a building downtown. To feel yourself as a historical being is to feel that your individual fate is attenuated, a bit submerged, in comparison to your existence as part of a collective. This is the feeling DeLillo successfully and at times overwhelmingly evokes.

3

So far I've been trying to get across *Underworld's* overall effect. I've wanted to suggest the way it contains, and evokes, our modern awareness of history.

But this risks making the book sound schematic. It isn't. You don't just travel through *Underworld*. You live in it. It's true that DeLillo isn't afraid of being an essayist, of saying things. He is a public writer, interested in the contemporary world. But he has also developed a formidable power to evoke the texture of different lives, to give people voices, to show them interacting — and to do it all with a steely, rough prose full of the hard sound of American life — a quick prose, exact and laconic and a terrific pleasure to read sentence by sentence.

What especially excites in this book is the way actual history mixes with the history DeLillo has invented. Something hard to describe appears in *Underworld* which before now I'd found only in a kind of cartoon version in the novels of James Ellroy. I'm referring to the actual atmosphere of the past fifty years in the United States: black-humoured, nightmarish, amphetamine-driven, stunningly complex.

Every review of the book that I've read has noted the great sequences in which DeLillo brings the comedian Lenny Bruce to life. What makes these sequences so absorbing isn't just how they put Bruce in front of you; what also engrosses you is the way the whole atmosphere of the early sixties — that period during the Cuban missile crisis the year before John Kennedy was shot — is resurrected like a kind of glowing historical plasma. Here's a small piece:

> He did the opening again, checking the line for style and fit.

"Good evening, my fellow citizens."

A stir of renewed anticipation — maybe they wanted him to pursue the presidential thing, but he waved it off again and stood there sort of humming at the hips, doing a little wobble that seemed to get the next thought going.

Then he did the shrillest sort of falsetto.

"We're all gonna die!"

This cracked him up. He bent from the waist laughing and seemed to be using the mike as a geiger counter, waving it over the floorboards.

"Dig it, JFK's got this Russian man-bull staring him down, they're pizzle to pizzle, and this is a guy Jack doesn't know how to deal with. What's he supposed to say? I shtupped more debutantes than you? This is a coal miner, he's a guy who herded farm animals barefoot for a couple of kopeks. He's been known to stick his fist up a sow's ass to fertilize his vegetable garden. What's Jack suppose to say to him — a secretary gave me a handjob on the White House elevator? This is a guy who craps with the door open on state occasions. He has sex with his bowling trophies."

DeLillo captures perfectly the way Bruce would improvise — the way he'd lurch along, getting caught on a line, a sentence, another line, until finally he found his bit. And because he brings Bruce's spiel so fully to life, he also evokes, in an almost uncanny way, that coffee-and-sugar sweatiness, that hard-talking, hey-guy atmosphere of the early sixties that Bruce floated in. You can hear Frank Sinatra and the Rat Pack in Bruce's bits; you can hear Dean Martin drawling to an interviewer about the great dump he had that afternoon.

Still, for me the finest prose in the book comes near the end. In Part 6 DeLillo takes the reader through the Fordham section of the Bronx where he lived as a young man. It's 1951 again. And DeLillo's mastery of dialogue, the wiry moodiness of his sentences are electrified by a new intensity. He is exploring Nick Shay's youth, and as he takes Nick through the streets, listening to people, catching the cool, passionate feeling of those days, the reader can't help but think that he's returning to his own young manhood. Whatever, this is the best writing DeLillo's done.

4

Underworld is about the United States — or to give it its legendary name, America. Reading it, responding to it, I realized the degree to which American culture is my culture. At the same time I realized the smaller but decisive degree to which it isn't.

Here in Canada, more maybe than in any other country in the world, the American cultural empire has enforced a strange bifocal vision. We "see American" in the middle and long distance — in our news and entertainment; and in the near distance, in our interactions with each other and the natural world, we "see Canadian." I don't know if this phenomenon can be called colonial. Maybe some other word would be more accurate.

But I do know it's real. And because *Underworld* is, among other things, a great essay on the United States, it challenged me to think about Canada and the literature we currently produce. My first thought was: Why don't we have books with this density and force? And immediately the answer came to me: We don't have them because we're a small country, lacking the conflicts — and the interest — generated by an imperial power. But it also struck me that because we "see American," the world we actually live in doesn't grip us — we seem to be unable to imaginatively take hold of our own life.

A couple of years ago I saw the Warner/Dreamworks movie *Deep Impact* which was playing at the Granville Cineplex downtown. Sharon and I were comfortably seated at the edge of the row. The audience was just right: not so big we felt crowded, but not so small we felt lonely. We watched the Eaton's ad, a fast montage of disgusted girls putting on clothes that the rest of the world wanted them to wear. Not bad. Then came the trailers, loud and fast, one advertising *The Newton Show*.

All right. I grabbed a handful of popcorn. This was fine. The hors d'oeuvres were being served and in a moment the feature banquet would start. Then — incredibly — the National Film Board logo filled the screen.

Old-fashioned fiddle music started to play and the NFB logo gave way to a pencil and watercolour animation of a kid walking jerkily down a country road. His feet didn't quite touch the ground.

Somebody in the audience hissed. Opening credits rolled. The short — because of course it would be a short — was "The Sweater," yet another version of the Roch Carrier memoir. "Get it off!" somebody muttered.

I felt embarrassed. I was ashamed to have this old-fashioned piece of Cancult inserted into the show we were watching.

As it turned out, the piece wasn't bad. But as soon as it ended, and the animated helicopter swooped howling through the ultramodern city, letting us know we were listening to DTS sound, the effect of the short died away and we were back in the world of real entertainment.

Reading *Underworld* made me reflect not just on the surreal power of the United States. It also made me think of that country's gravity, its density, the way, like a giant star bending rays of light, it distorts and alters everything around it. DeLillo's achievement lies in the fact that he has produced an analogue of his nation, an object whose heft and complexity, far from being overdone, are in fact just barely sufficient for their purpose.

A Canadian book of similar scope — what would it read like? Oddly, for me, the one book that comes to mind right now is Seth's great graphic novel *Clyde Fans – Part One*. In this heartbreaking, yet immensely rich graphic work (and we only have half of it!), the bright, lonely air of Canada, which casts such black shadows on the sidewalks and on the sides of buildings, which makes the loose threads of toques shimmer in the light – this bright clear air contrasts at the deepest possible level with the skies rimmed with carbon down which American jets roar everywhere in DeLillo's book. The difference in the air we breathe and the light on our faces: by showing it to us, Seth has achieved something greater than it might seem, for it reminds us of a different ethical dimension that shimmers beneath our apparent similarity, and of how often fate – which is another name for what cannot be denied or wished away – colours the Canadian air.

Vermeer's Patch

1

I want to start by right away giving some sense of the scope of Northrop Frye's two studies of the Bible, *The Great Code* and *Words with Power*. Read with care, their effect is surreal, so let me use a surreal image: compared to most literary criticism, the books appear like two pyramids rising out of the plains.

2

Frye treats the Bible as a book instead of as a collection of discrete texts. And he does so because he finds that it coheres as a structure of words. This coherence Frye calls the Bible's typological pattern and a large part of his writing on the Bible is concerned with it.

You quickly see why: once the pattern is recognized the whole Bible seems transformed, revealing an order remarkable in its scope and pervasiveness. From the level of individual characters to the level of overall form, Frye's Bible is dominated by a principle which is maybe most familiar to us in the call-and-response pattern of work songs and religious meetings. One statement (the type) is answered by another (the antitype); the result is both a powerful sense of communion and a powerful sense of order

— powerful because the call and response pattern produces a self-enclosed world, a kind of double mirror in which language reverberates as it moves back and forth and so becomes a group voice instead of a collection of individual voices.

This group voice Frye finds everywhere in the Bible. He discovers it even when its individual components are separated by vast gulfs of space or time. From the level of structure (the Old Testament calling out to the New, the Book of Genesis calling out to the Book of Revelation) to the level of stories (the saving of mankind from the Flood corresponding to Christian baptism, the evil city of Rome to wicked Babylon), typology figures everywhere in the Bible.

3

Three consequences ensue.

First, to read the Bible rightly you should read it aloud. The call-and-response structure of typology not only foregoes the sequential nature of modern prose (the way it unrolls like a thread on a bobbin); it also foregoes modern prose's silence. Public and ceremonious, the Bible's language asks to be *voiced*. This explains why its segments are numbered; it explains why it contains highlighted words showing where spoken emphasis should go; and it explains why to the modern reader the Bible seems so archaic.

Second, the Bible's typology induces a very special conception of history. Just as Christ is the antitype or realized form of Adam, and the New Testament the antitype or realization of the Old, so those who are saturated with typological rhetoric will perceive the future as a realization of the past and the past as a prefiguration of the future.

In other words, typology isn't just a form of rhetoric. It is also a mode of thinking that structures time. The type exists in the past and the antitype in the present; or, alternatively, the type exists in the present and the antitype in the years to come.

Thus for those who have a typological cast of mind a deeply

comforting order exists which has nothing to do with causation, the thing usually associated with historical change. And this is true whether what is being considered is the existence of the individual or the existence of mankind. In the case of the individual, the type of life here on earth will have its antitype in a life thereafter; in the case of mankind, the type of the present will be realized in an antitypal time to come.

This cast of mind Frye finds especially noticeable in Marxism. But to bring up Marxism is to bring up the third and revolutionary consequence of Biblical typology — the *theory* of history it poses.

4

A self-enclosed world, the Bible provides a representation of existence stretching from creation to the end of time. In a sense there is nothing outside its double mirror — the Beginning is reflected in the End and the End in the Beginning. This makes the Bible autonomous (it stands by itself and refers to nothing outside itself); but it also makes it global (it contains everything). These characteristics become especially interesting when you consider the Bible's relationship to science fiction. The tremendous yearning in science fiction for a visionary complement to history — or rather to the nightmare which the causal conception of history has placed on humanity's chest — has led it to be dismissed as an escapist, marginal form. Yet taken as a whole, science fiction is nothing less than the Bible secularized.

Think of the famous cut in the movie *2001: A Space Odyssey* in which the type of the bone thrown into the air yields to the antitype of the docking spaceship. As so often in science fiction, these two images that reflect each other, that call out to each other, are connected causally only in the most superficial way. What is really at work here is a kind of magic, in which instead of endlessly unrolling, like a wound-up thread, history suddenly unfolds, like a blossom. And it is the double mirror of typology that both here and in the Bible makes this sudden blossoming of history realizable.

Now, by representing time and space as it does, the Bible simultaneously miniaturizes the universe and subjects it in its entirety to narrative — the very process which distinguishes science fiction. More importantly, in doing so it holds out the promise of an end to history, an apotheosis which is to be humanity's permanent and ever-renewed consolation.

Again and again Frye alludes to this. This is where the Bible becomes revolutionary, he says, where it promises a definite point at which earthbound time stops and Paradisical time begins. Permeated with the image of Eden, this promise shows us a cosmos which is no longer subservient to the pain of history but instead is in complicity with liberated man; and it is this very promise — hungrily seized on by its readers — which surfaces in science fiction today. Narratives of the future that end with the transfiguration of humanity and the replacement of history by cosmic time are at the heart of the genre, and it seems to me no accident that a number of its works — all those three- and four-volume epic series — have tried to achieve the same all-encompassing quality which characterizes their precursor.

I mention all this for one reason. Frye is drawn to the Bible precisely by the gargantuan hope it proposes. Though he was no Communist, Frye had at least this much in common with that other great twentieth-century literary critic, Walter Benjamin: his reading of the Bible (and indeed of literature and human work in general) was entirely bound up with the concept of redemption. From his study of Blake on, the image of a redeemed mankind was central to Frye's work. And his studies of the Bible aren't exceptions. In the final analysis they are visionary books. True, their arguments are substantial. A more subtle and tenacious reading would be hard to imagine. Yet time and again Frye's thinking brings to mind Pope's great couplet:

> Thence, by a soft transition, we repair
> From earthly vehicles to those of air

as in mid-page and sometimes in mid-sentence he lifts off from a concrete examination of his subject to what seems like less a reading of the Bible than a meditation on what the Bible points to: a vision of humanity no longer lost in the hell it has made for itself.

5

Now I want to refer the reader to Philip Marchand, the influential Toronto book reviewer, and in particular to Marchand's dismissal of Frye a few years back as "unrealistic." In his much-publicized book *Ripostes: Reflections on Canadian Literature* (you may remember it for its attacks on Atwood, Ondaatje, et al.), Marchand wrote as a disciple of John Metcalf. But while Metcalf puts on a flamboyant act, slashing his Zorro-like mark into the stony wall of Canlit, Marchand resembles the awkward boy who has made it to the big desk and now sits impassive behind it, exerting his authority by making sure that feelings of exuberance, outrage or delight never appear.

Not that he doesn't express opinions; you couldn't ask for a more judgemental book. But his lips barely move. When Marchand turns to Northrop Frye and his two books on the Bible this prissiness becomes offensive. He patronizes Frye, treating him as a kind of effete mandarin who suggests "that it is slightly vulgar or unsophisticated for anyone even to raise the issue of what 'really happened'" when it comes to the events described in the Bible. Reviewing *Words with Power*, the second of Frye's two studies of the Bible, Marchand sarcastically sums up Frye's viewpoint :

> So, to get to the nub of the matter, the question of whether the God of the Bible really exists — or, as Frye might put it, "really exists" — is silly. Of course, He exists. You can imagine Him, can't you? The whole of *Words with Power* is an argument that a reader's imaginative absorption into the myth and metaphors of the Bible leads to the dissolving of the "antithesis between a human subject and a divine object." ...

The argument ... will not be convincing to those who believe that reality is even richer than the human imagination. This may seem a bizarre or trivial example, but at one point, while reading *Words with Power*, I thought of the case of Elvis Presley — a mythical, almost godlike figure in the making, if one can judge by his omnipresent icons. If a chronicle of Presley's life were preserved for generations hence, what would the Northrop Frye critic make of it? Such a critic would note that Presley had a twin brother who died at birth, and probably say, as Frye does in *Words with Power*, that the twin motif, applied to heroes and gods, runs all through folklore and literature. ...

There is a great deal more that this Frye critic could do with the life of Presley. All of it would amount, in the end, to less than the fact of Presley's existence, to the terrible importance of a life that "really happened." Christians no doubt feel the same way, in a case of infinitely greater moment, about Frye's treatment of Jesus.

"The argument ... will not be convincing to those who believe that reality is even richer than the human imagination." Marchand makes two mistakes here. First, he assumes that Frye wasn't interested in reality — in what "really happened" or happens. Second, he assumes that he knows better than Frye how the imagination relates to reality, something which especially shows itself in his pompous final paragraph, in which he implies that Frye treats Christian belief frivolously.

I've emphasized this passage because it shows the pettiness of Marchand's sense of the imagination. Here, as so often in current book reviewing, a flabby journalistic realism rules. Frye had an enormous range of interests. Like Walter Benjamin, his thinking on literature was grounded in scholarship. And for exactly this reason — and again, like Benjamin — he concluded that the relationship of art to reality was far more complicated — far deeper — than that suggested by the kind of realism Marchand favours.

Marcel Proust felt this too. A scholar in his own way, and a brilliant observer of reality, Proust remained, like Frye and Benjamin, an idealist. In *The Captive*, the fifth volume of his great book, Bergotte, suffering from an attack of uremia, looks again at Vermeer's little patch of yellow wall. Proust writes: "He was not unconscious of the gravity of his condition. In a celestial pair of scales there appeared to him, weighing down one of the pans, his own life, while the other contained the little patch of wall so beautifully painted in yellow. He felt that he had rashly sacrificed the former for the latter."

A few minutes later Bergotte suffers a fresh attack of uremia. He rolls to the floor from the circular settee he has sunk down on; attendants and other visitors come hurrying to his assistance. "He was dead," Proust writes.

> Dead for ever? Who can say? ... All we can say is that everything is arranged in this life as though we entered it carrying the burden of obligations contracted in a former life; there is no reason inherent in the conditions of life on this earth that can make us consider ourselves obliged to do good, to be fastidious, to be polite even, nor make the talented artist consider himself obliged to begin over again a score of times a piece of work the admiration aroused by which will matter little to his body devoured by worms, like the patch of yellow wall painted with so much knowledge and skill by an artist who must for ever remain unknown and who is barely identified under the name Vermeer. All these obligations, which have no sanction in our present life, seem to belong to a different world, founded upon kindness, scrupulosity, self-sacrifice, a world entirely different from this, which we leave in order to be born into this world, before perhaps returning to the other to live once again beneath the sway of those unknown laws which we obeyed because we bore their precepts in our hearts, knowing not whose hand had traced them there — those laws to which every profound work of the intellect brings us nearer and which are invisible only — and still! — to fools.

Marchand cannot understand this. Though he kow-tows to Frye's "brilliance," he clearly thinks him a dreamer. Running with the herd, he sniggers at Frye; he scoffs at the great critic for not being more like himself.

Like other book reviewers before him (and, no doubt, others who will come after him), Marchand presents Frye as a mandarin, too precious to matter on the street. Yet when I go into Chris Brayshaw's Pulpfiction book store and watch the teenagers and older men and women like myself as we review the science fiction and the rows of poetry and avant-garde literature, I know that the comforting presence at our sides isn't Marchand; it is Frye. He understands our need for wonder, for the excessive, unprecedented image in which the true surrealistic face of existence breaks through. He knows what literature is for.

Leetle Bateese

1

One afternoon about ten years ago I was talking to the five-ton driver at Postal Station D in Vancouver. We started talking about writing. Roy asked me if I was working on anything. I said I was thinking about William Henry Drummond's "Habitant" poems, which were written around the turn of the century. I had recently started reading them, I said; and I'd been amazed at how entire sections of my childhood were preserved in their lines.

But Roy couldn't get the reference.

Finally I said, "You know. Leetle Bateese."

"Oh, right! Right! Leetle Bateese! 'Leetle Bateese, you bad leetle boy.' I remember that. I read that when I was a kid."

In the next two months I talked to maybe a dozen people about Drummond. I found that about half remembered reading him in school; three or four people hadn't heard of him at all, and one person confused him with the inventor of Paul Bunyan and his blue ox Babe. But in general I received enthusiastic responses. Like popular songs and advertising jingles, it seemed that Drummond's poetry stuck in one's brain.

But while Drummond was the only turn-of-the-century Canadian poet I knew of who was remembered like this, his writing had disappeared from the curriculum. He wasn't discussed even as part of Canadian literary history. B.W. Powe spoke for most when he wrote: "Add further complications: a place without a flag to identify as its own, whose 'Literature' (it cannot be called writing yet) is either imported or institutionalized, where someone can poeticize

> Dere's somet'ing stirrin' my blood tonight,
> On de night of de young new year,
> W'ile de camp is warm an' de fire is bright,
> An' de bottle is close at han' . . .

and it could be considered a part of the national treasury." Powe here quotes Drummond's "The Voyager", and it's plain that he is using Drummond to epitomize everything parochial, old-fashioned and corny about Canadian writing.

Which is fair enough. Drummond is corny. If you were to compile a *Canuck Bumper Book* (its cover wreathed in toques and moose antlers, say), his poems would probably fill about a third of it. No other Canadian poet before or since has been so vulgar. But since he is *spectacularly* out of date, why not discuss him? After all, every other Canadian writer who might have even the faintest claim on our attention has been resuscitated in the past two decades. (I know: I've attended classes on Canadian writers who to all extents and purposes were unreadable.) What does Drummond have wrong that these writers don't?

Well, he was a bigot. Open any collection of Drummond's poems and a concentrated blast of stereotypes hits you in the face. It starts with the lines of dialect themselves, whose vowel-consonant combinations are saturated with the pure dumb nasal *ho ho* of the Jean Chretien character on "Air Farce" (" 'Yass-yass,' I say, 'mebbe you t'ink I'm wan beeg loup garou'"), and it goes on from there to build up a world as swollen with popular mythology as the world of "The Beverly Hillbillies." Like Vachel Lindsay's "The Congo," Drummond's writing *embarrasses*. Read his poems, and you are back in the world of "The Happy Nigger" and "The Pigtail of Wu Fu Li."

Yet what most embarrasses me about his verse is how familiar it is. I have just reread all the "Habitant" poems; and I don't think I exaggerate when I say that the mental image most English Canadians have of Quebeckers is still largely the one propagated by Drummond.

No wonder so many Quebecois hate us! Everything Drummond ladles onto the plate — the playfulness, the toques, the Saturday soirees with their fiddle music, the enormous families, the sheepishness, the bad education – the *dumbness*, really — all this remains part of the mythology of French Canada so far as the English are concerned. Read Drummond's poems – right away you feel as if the anti-French prejudice that gets bleached out of the Anglo in our cultural washing machines is reappearing before your eyes. If you're like me, you'll settle into the writing with the same bemused emotions one might feel listening to a seventy-year-old uncle talk about getting Jewed down by the Chink grocers in Edmonton.

Not that Drummond preaches hate. His verse is sweet. But he was saturated in the prejudices of his day. As a result, his poems now seem almost grotesquely sentimental. Nor is this sentimentality confined to their "leetle guy" attitude, all those *gran-peres* who'd rather be poor and 'appy than rich and corrupt like the Yank. It goes deeper.

In the best of our own popular art — in movies and rap songs — the deprived Other is at least seen as tough. In Drummond's verse, though, the illiterate farmers and loggers are completely stripped of their virility. They become children — so much so that when you're reading the poems in their original format and come across one of Frederick Coburn's illustrations of rawboned, serious men, you feel a shock: you expect little round fellows with apple cheeks. In the following, for example, I grimaced not just at the horrific size of the family (which helped me understand why Quebec women now have almost the lowest birthrates in the world); I also grimaced at the smarmy, placating, Norman Rockwell chuckle:

Ma fader an' ma moder too, got nice, nice familee,

Dat's ten garcon an' t'orteen girl, was mak' it twenty
    t'ree
But fonny t'ing de Gouvernement don't geev de firs'
    prize den
Lak w'at dey say dey geev it now, for only wan
    douzaine
De English peep dat only got wan familee small size
Mus' be feel glad dat tam dere is no honder acre prize
For fader of twelve chil'ren-dey know dat mus' be so,
De Canayens would boss Kebeck — mebbe Ontario.
But dat is not de story dat I was gone tole you
About de fun we use to have w'en we leev a chez nous

Drummond's master was Kipling. But I can't imagine Kipling's soldiers saying those last two lines. His Cockneys with their stunted legs might have bowed to the social order, but Kipling never presented them as ass lickers. He accepted his subjects for what they were in a way that Drummond did not.

2

So why has Drummond endured? He was a bigot and a senti-mentalist; he turned the unblinking anger of the Quebecois into treacle. So why does he — like Pauline Johnson and Robert Ser-vice — still last in some way, while other writers who are far more favoured by the academy go unread? Why does Roy Bernard, a literate five-ton driver at Canada Post, still remember lines from his work? And why does Leetle Bateese, a tough square-shaped figure with the manic energy of the Katzenjammer Kids, haunt my dreams, almost like a member of my extended family?

The answer is complicated. But right away one thing has to be noticed: exactly where Drummond is at his most embarrass-ing he becomes most vital. In his use of Habitant patois Drum-mond tapped into a current which I want to argue is now much more important than the Tennysonian-Romantic flow found in the poetry of his peers — a current that remains alive, and in fact is the chief source of energy in modern poetry, in all the various places that modern poetry can be found. I have in mind what might roughly be described as the replacement of the voice of the individual with the voice of the crowd, the mass public; and maybe the best way to evoke this aspect of Drummond's verse is through quotation.

Below I've listed four pieces of writing: three by the "Confederation poets" who were Drummond's peers — Bliss Carman, D.C. Scott and Archibald Lampman — and one by Drummond. All of them deal with nature (which is one of the bigger themes of the Habitant poems, and probably the theme of the more artistic, "Canadian" poetry that the Confederation poets were trying to write). Bliss Carman first:

> Was it a year or lives ago
> We took the grasses in our hands
> And caught the summer flying low
> Over the waving meadow lands,
> And held it here between our hands?

D.C. Scott:

> A storm cloud was marching
> Vast on the prairie,
> Scored with livid ropes of hail,
> Quick with nervous vines of lightning —

Archibald Lampman:

> Where the far elm-tree shadows flood
> Dark patches in the burning grass,
> The cows, each with her peaceful cud,
> Lie waiting for the heat to pass.
> From somewhere on the slope near by
> Into the pale depth of the noon
> A wandering thrush slides leisurely
> His thin revolving tune.

And finally Drummond:

> An' down on de reever de wil' duck is quackin'
> Along by de shore leetle san' piper ronne —
> De bullfrog he's gr-rompin' an' dore is jumpin' —
> Dey all got der own way for mak' it de fonne.

To drive the difference home, I quote part of a ballad by Carman:

> On the long, slow heave of a lazy sea,
> To the flap of an idle sail,
> The Nancy's Pride went out on the tide;
> And the skipper stood by the rail . . .

And part of one by Drummond:

> On wan dark night on Lac St. Pierre,
> De win' she blow, blow, blow,
> An de crew of de wood scow 'Julie Plante'
> Got scar't an' run below —
> For de win' she blow lak hurricane
> Bimeby she blow some more,
> An de' scow bus' up on Lac St. Pierre
> Wan arpent from de shore.

I could go on, but these passages ought to show the vigour that Drummond got into his work. Drummond discovered the power of *spoken* language, the fact that it carries with it all the atmosphere of the situations in which it is used. He discovered that once you let bits of common speech into your verse — "gr-romping," say, or "bus' up on Lac St. Pierre" — the writing immediately gains bite and tactility. And he discovered that the use of such speech lightens the verse's Poetic Solemnity: you hear a man speaking, not an intoning artificer.

This gives the verse life. But even more, it puts the writer on the side of his audience. Common, everyday speech is what we use to touch others, after all, the kind of speech that goes along with arm gestures and a warm tone of voice. So that by using an intensely colloquial language, Drummond immediately gains a sense of vivacity and ease.

By contrast, look at what his peers were doing. The painful fact is that the harder Lampman and the rest strained to write in a "pure" language not stained with the dirt of common use, the more their poetry was emptied of any sense of a natural voice, of that idiosyncratic yet instantly recognizable syntax that you find in Tennyson or Whitman, for instance.

Drummond, to be sure, wasn't able to suggest a specific individual either. Quebec patois was too far from his own English. Nevertheless, the fact that his verse used the fluent *spoken* phrase instead of the constructed sentence or line allowed him to develop a persona through which he could freely express his emotions (something none of the Confederation poets were able to do). It also allowed him to use the new vocabulary that at least one section of the Canadian world had developed for itself and so to bring that world into written existence in a direct way.

All this contributed to his success. In the end, though, what brought him his truly enormous popularity — and at the height of his fame no poet in the English-speaking world was better known — what brought him his fame was his ungrudging, almost pulp-magazine willingness to give his readers what they wanted. He offered them a Canada that was wild but still softened by social use, a legendary country where the loon cried and the paddle dipped and voyageurs in red wool sashes lived under the signs of the birch bark canoe and the Sacred Heart of Jesus.

Lampman and Scott had written as solitaries; they had described a landscape seen by a man alone, undomesticated by communal experience. But Drummond placed communal experience at the heart of his poetry. He crowded his verse with people; his wilderness glowed with storybook colours. And so for his original audience, at least, he vivified and made human what otherwise would have been just a cold space on the map.

3

Drummond was a limited poet. Because he had to rely on a con-strained vocabulary, he could only do a few things well. Read a lot of him and you realize that his poems have that sameness which afflicts all commercial mass culture and which comes from the need to give the public exactly what it wants, again and again and again.

At the same time, how much of Canadian mythology derives from this writer! Poutine, toques, checked shirts, beaver and moose, fiddle music, "ouaih, ouaih," and "tabernac" — we laugh; but we like it too. The fact is, Drummond's work has an unmistakable vitality. It has that iconic toughness that marks cartoon characters like Donald Duck. It "lives." You can't help but respond to its verve, its slambang rhythms:

> Ax dem along de reever
> Ax dem along de shore
> Who was de mos' bes' fightin' man
> From Managance to Shaw-in-i-gan?
> De place w'ere de great beeg rapide roar,
> Johnnie Courteau!

Along with the rhythmic strength of his writing, how much sensuous data his poems contain compared to those of the Con-federation poets! Look at his proper names, for instance, which to my ears evoke all the poetry of old Quebec:

> Dere was Telesphore Montbriand, Paul Desjardins,
>   Louis Guyon,
> Bill McKeever, Aleck Gauthier, an' hees cousin Jean
>   Bateese

And consider his use of the various Quebecois terms for birds and other animals — *dore*, *gou-glou* — and also his precise feel-

ing for the seasons which is shared by people who live a lot outside — spring, for instance:

> W'en small sheep is firs' comin' out on de pasture,
> Deir nice leetle tail stickin' out on deir back

Then there are the descriptions of men at work, the talk around
the stove, the bits of conversation heard out in the field, all of it
made vivid by the very thing Drummond is attacked for — that
mixture of French and English that allowed him to bypass his
over-refinement of feeling and respond directly to the world in
front of him.

4

Well, all this is fine, you might say. But what about the *embarrassment* of Drummond? What about those ass-licking farmers
and cow-eyed Philomenes? Aren't they sufficient reason to keep
him off the curriculum?

I would argue that they are not. In fact, I would argue that
we ought to have Drummond in the curriculum at least in part
because of those farmers and Philomenes. If we want to really
feel our literature as a living thing, it won't do just to glance with
distaste at E.J. Pratt and A.J.M. Smith (those wooden initials,
those tongue depressers!). We also ought to read Pauline Johnson's poems and Ernest Thompson Seton's animal stories; we
ought to know the vast "frontier" literature of BC and Alberta,
and at least one or two of those books like Gene Stratton Porter's
Freckles which defined Canada to the world for at least a third of
the century just past. And why not look at the poems of the hard-
eyed British Empire jingoists who used to fill the anthologies, or
the old *Star Weekly* writers like Greg Scott? A true national literature isn't just a sequence of masterpieces. It is a spectrum of
things that in the case of Canada ranges from Margaret Avison's
poems to the writing of Harold "Sonny" Ladoo, from *The Dan-
gerous River* to *Breaking Smith's Quarterhorse*, from *Regards et*

jeux dans l'espace to the anti-Semitic columns in the thirties *Le Devoir.*

The truth of our past is the most exciting thing about it. And like other exciting things it will sometimes embarrass and even shame us. Drummond is part of that truth. He makes us flush even as he gives pleasure; he makes us recognize that sometimes we can hold two viewpoints at once when looking at a writer's work.

The great thing is to read him ironically. And with enjoyment. I remember loving "Leetle Bateese" as a boy; and I see that poem now as something that belongs to me, along with the Quebec fairy tales I grew up with and the stories I thrilled to about the great journeys of Henry Kelsey and la Verendrye, where for the first time I caught glimpses of a world I would find again much later, when I was fully grown and was looking (with urgency now) for a landscape that contained bears and horses and people who were at home with them.

The Light on the Tracks
Part One

1

Ashcroft is a desert village located on the banks of the Thompson River. It's about ten kilometres from Cache Creek. Two railroads run through it — Canadian National and Canadian Pacific. Twenty-four hours a day big yellow trucks rumble down the steep Highland Valley road and unload copper ore into cars running on the CP line. In July and August the temperature can climb above 40 degrees. The mesas rising up from the river become bleached-looking, and only the irrigated fields of the nearby ranches give the eye a place to rest. A number of Native reserves are located in the area, strung out along Highway 97 between Big Horn and Twenty Mile. I had come to Ashcroft to learn about the relations between Natives and whites, but I was shy, and for the first few weeks the residents of the motel where I was staying took up my time.

Three of these residents became for me like attendant spirits, fairy tale figures, semi-magical, something like the mechanics in Shakespeare's plays. Of the three, Wayne Cochrane was the most important. He would introduce me to people and open up the town for me. He would make me think anything was possible. At the same time he made me wary. He was a bright person; he had grown up among people he could trick. Often his speech danced around a subject as if to hide it from view.

164

Yet he had a humble heart, and I came to see that his brightness had done him no good. His openness and eagerness led him to cross social boundaries — in doing so, he upset people. And when I finally left town two months later I saw in him a kind of double of myself, a more desperate and less proud alter-self, an unhappy Ariel in whose urgent voice I had learned to hear pathos.

I met him about four days after I arrived. One night I heard an insistent rap on my window; when I opened the door, a small handsome man stared at me.

"Hello?"

"Hello! Are you the guy that's writin' about cowboys and the west?"

"I guess so."

"That's great! That's neat!"

"Do I know you?"

"No, but we gotta talk. I heard from Cec, Cecil, the guy you were talkin' to? that you were interested in cowboys. Well I'm a cowboy. My name's Wayne Cochrane. So what about it? You wanna come over and talk?"

"Sure."

"That's great!"

Right away I saw that I had never met anyone like him. He sat across from me in his room drinking coffee — "You want some? You sure?" — dressed in jeans and a white shirt, a little gold stud in his ear, a delicate gold chain around his neck with a cross hanging from it, a bit of a fancy man with his fine jaw and clipped rancher's mustache, but above all excitable, hectic, talking in a quick, high-pitched voice and staring at me with anxious eyes that made me think of the eyes of a beautiful East Indian woman telling her lover he would have to go.

He overwhelmed me. Each question I asked worked like a squirt of gasoline on a fire. He talked for well over two hours — about his young years when he had first lived in Ashcroft, about motorcycles, Prince George, Prince Rupert, unions, Gene Autry, his wonderful kids, a poem he had written to his daughter, horses, how to get a welding ticket, rifles versus handguns, why driving truck was so hard, and nicknames. Then all at once he leaned forward. "God, Bruce, I can hardly tell you what it means to me talkin' to you like this. I'm in my glory, Sir Bruce, and that's no lie."

2

It was still May. But the next morning when I stepped out of my room into the quiet and heat I had all that old summer feeling.

My three fairy-tale figures, Wayne and Ray and Max — Ray a Native man, Max an immense, soft-voiced white man and Ray's next-door neighbour (Max had a club foot that he showed me one day – it looked like the hoof of a cow) — were sitting in the shaded chairs lined up outside my door. Ray sat closest to me.

"Hey Raymond," I said.

He bolted upright, a small tubby man with angry eyes.

I held up my hands. "I'm sorry I scared you."

"I wasn't scared."

"I don't smell any poop," Max said.

"C'mere. Have a cigarette," Ray said.

I stepped forward and took the cigarette he offered and pointed at the box Max was holding in his lap. "What you got there?"

"Fishing gear." His soft voice had a boudoir intimacy in the otherwise silent morning. He opened up the little box in his lap. "Pretty nice eh?"

"Beautiful," Wayne said, and slurped coffee from a big, silver, thermos-like cup. "I like the little shelves. I never was much for fishing, but huntin' — now I like to hunt, I like guns, period. Like I've got my —" he rummaged in the pack at his feet and to my amazement he took out a handgun. It was futuristic-looking: a pistol with a space-age grip in matte black and a slightly flat-tened barrel with an attached sight.

"Jesus Christ, Wayne," I said. "That's a gun."

He grinned. "Hey, not so loud eh. We don't wanna get the RCMP here."

Max stared at the gun. "Is that thing loaded? Holy crow, I can see the bullet in the cylinder there."

"Don't worry, there's two safeties on it," Wayne said.

Ray said: "That's real."

I said: "If there's anything you want, like just tell me now, just let me know."

"Bruce. Don't worry. I can show you. I got three handguns in here right now."

"Three eh." I felt upset. "That's a fuck of a lot of guns for one guy just in a motel room."

"Listen Sir Bruce, they're legal, you know. Everything's legal."

"But why are you carrying guns?"

"What do you mean?"

"Just what I said. Why are you carrying guns?"

"Oh for Christ's sake!" He glared at me. Then, frightening and astonishing me, he stood up and waved the gun in my face. "So you're one of those guys that believes in gun control eh? You know sir I thought you were smarter than that. I really did. I thought you understood how things were. But you know what? People don't want to face facts. They don't give a shit whether I own a rifle or a BB gun. They talk about some little old lady who's lost a son in a shooting accident or some guy who's gone berserk, but it's all bullshit. What they really want is to have the nation disarm. That's what they fuckin' want."

"Wayne, stop waving that thing at me."

"You worried about this? Fucking handgun? Listen to me now. I got friends, they got weapons that are superior to military weapons other than guided missiles, you know that? I got people in Prince Rupert who've greased handguns and rifles and buried them in the ground along with ammunition so it'll last a thousand years because they're worried about what can happen. Because of the government. Because of fucking gun control!"

Max shook his head. Wayne glared at him, crouching a little, holding the gun as if at any second he might fire on this white-whiskered man looking up at him. Ray held up a hand. "Wayne. Stop waving that thing. Don't look at Max like that. Just hold on a sec. I want to ask you a question. Okay? Okay?"

"Okay."

"What's in that coffee of yours?"

"What?"

"You on some drug? You sound like it."

3

There was the gun; and a few days later there was the bed. We were walking up Railway under the cloudless sky to have eggs and toast. All at once Wayne turned to me: "Dear Sir Bruce, you're gonna hate me for this, you're just gonna wanna kill me, but I got a favour to ask of you."

"Ask away sir."

"I wanna borrow your bed for next Saturday."

"What?"

"Bev's comin'. That girlfriend I told you about? And my bed smells! It stinks of tobacco! It's awful! I can't have her lyin' on that bed with me, she'll think I'm just a bum. And I know you got a good bed, so I'm asking you sir to do me this favour."

"Wayne, I told you my wife's coming up this weekend. Jesus Christ, you know that."

"Yeah, but she's your wife. You get to see her all the time. How often do I get to see Bev?"

4

That Wednesday Wayne caught me talking to Sharon on the motel's public phone. He wanted a turn. He kept staring at me through the glass, I couldn't tell why. He was too polite to ask how long I was going to be. Finally, excited, his hand cupped over his mouth, he said, "Gail called!"

I thought: Who's Gail?

5

"Gail might be comin' to visit."

"Is that good news or bad?"

"Well, I'll tell you sir I don't know."

He was helping me move my last few things upstairs. (My new unit was a hundred dollars less that than the one I'd been staying in on the ground floor.) Gail, it turned out, was a Christian woman whom he'd met through a correspondence club. She was in an unhappy marriage. She had fallen in love with him. Even better, she wanted to take care of him. The trouble was, she knew about Bev and Bev knew about her and neither liked the other.

And there was another problem. Wayne still lusted for Bev. "Gail's sweet; and she loves the hell outa me. But I can't . . . I'll tell ya, I'm caught in the middle here."

All the while he was helping me move, lugging my exercise bike up the stairs, my books, my packs, talking and gesticulating while Barry, a painfully thin stock clerk with red hair and a sun-damaged face who lived in the unit next to my new one, stood watching, his arms hanging down, blinking his eyes, wanting to help but not knowing how.

6

So there was Wayne; and there were the other residents of the Motel who made me feel at home. On the second floor landing one evening Ray and Max and Ray's friend Cecil (another Native and the first person I'd talked to in Ashcroft), were leaning against the railing looking out at the hills. It was evening and the hills were striped in their upper half in a layer of gold like an incandescent moss. Ray was smoking.

"We were talking about chain saws," Cecil said. "I was just saying how it takes nothing to hurt yourself with 'em."

"That's true."

"But as long as you don't get to your vital organs, you're okay," Max said. "If you can stop the bleeding you'll live."

"Hell, you don't need a chainsaw to damage your goddamn organs," Ray said. "I remember seein' this guy smoke a cigarette through a hole in his throat. Couldn't stop."

A silence.

"I'll tell you one thing," Max offered in his soft voice.

"What's that."

"If your liver packs up, the rest of your body's gonna follow."

"Yeah, well, if the asshole shuts down the rest of the body does too."

"Ha ha ha!" Max said. "Get a T-shirt made up: 'I'm an asshole and I'm important!'"

"You'd sell millions," I said.

Ray flicked his cigarette down onto the grass. "Where do you think that goddamn Hank is now?"

"He's out in the bush," Cecil said.

"You get hurt out there, boy."

Cecil nodded gravely. "I've known guys to go out and not come back. White and still, drained of their blood, dead ten hours."

"Well it can happen easy with a chain saw," I said.

"Hank isn't working with a saw," Max said. "He's movin' some cattle around. Up on the other side of Elephant Mountain there. Old Darryl came around askin' about him. Just after he took off. He knew where Hank had gone. He said he figured it would take Hank about thirty seconds to get packed."

"He loves that stuff," Cecil said.

"Anything to get on a horse. Anyway he'll be okay," Ray said. "Hank's got brains."

"I'll tell you who's a real brain," Max said. "Did you see that show on Stephen Hawking last night? Now there's a brain."

"Ah he's goddamn crippled all to hell," Ray said.

"He's still got his organs," I said.

Max glared at us. "You don't know what I'm saying. He's smart at a whole other level than anybody we know is smart. He just throws out ideas and other people try to figure out what he means."

"Different dimensions." Ray had heard it before.

"Hyperspace doesn't mean like on *Star Trek*. It means another dimension of space."

A train went by and we stopped talking. The empty black coal cars loped down the tracks, their sound deep and huge, filling the air, then fading into a muttering aftersound. In the renewed silence the wind in the cottonwoods sounded like the steady sigh of an ocean beach. The hills were shadowed now with stripes of grey and brown, and only at the top did they shine gold. Over the tracks and the road lay an even, calm, clear, grey light.

"Well, that's it for me," Cecil said, and went down the walkway to his room.

"Me too," Max said. "I'll talk to you girls tomorrow."

Ray nodded. "Sleep tight."

7

"He's good people. He just has these little sayings."

"You've known him long?"

"Fourteen years."

We smoked, lingering there at the railing.

8

"Take away your name. Who are you?"

"Interesting."

"Oh yeah."

He smoked. "'All the world's a stage' — how does that go?"

"'And the men upon it are merely players who strut and fret . . .'"

"Yeah. Where's that from."

"That's *Hamlet*. Shakespeare."

"He's got it right."

9

"Max has a bit of a temper," I said.

"Don't we all."

I nodded.

"I'm just learning control of myself now," Ray said. "I've got the same instincts in me as I've always had, but now I'm just learning to control them. If I'd known it was this damn hard to grow up I'd of died long ago. But what's growing up?"

"Good question."

"I'm too dumb to be a smart person. Too smart to be a dumb person. So I'm shit out of luck."

"Well, Ray, I don't know." I looked at him. He was staring out at the railroad tracks and the hills, his face dark in the dark.

"You raise a kid in a shitty environment, what do you expect. I can remember being in a situation when I was about eight or nine. I didn't want to fight. But I remember my old man saying, 'You get in there and fight.' It was either that or get a spanking. I remember thinking: This is shit."

He smoked. "AA and NA saved my life. I remember my dad getting drunk and beating up my mom — all that. I left home when I was twelve. Then I was put in a Catholic orphanage where they crammed religion down my throat and up my ass. What did I know. Nothing."

I wanted to ask him what tribe he was from, but I didn't dare. For some reason I thought he was from Saskatchewan. Maybe he was Cree. I said, "You've had an interesting life."

He frowned. "Interesting to you maybe."

We fell silent.

"I like to leave people alone, and I like to be left alone. Alone but not lonely."

We smoked together, our elbows on the balcony, looking at the blackness entering the trees and darkening the desert hills.

10

A week later when I stepped out of my unit I saw Cecil standing at the railing just outside my door. His arms were crossed and he was looking out across the parking lot. "I'm moving today," he said.

"But Cecil, I just got here!"

"Yeah, you just got here. I've been in this place two years. You think I should wait for you?"

He was dressed formally, in a black cowboy hat and black boots and stiff black Wrangler jeans and a black shirt with the cuffs rolled up once so that his wrists and wristwatch showed. Dressed this way,. with his paunch and stern dark face under the hat, he looked like a desperado going to be sentenced in court.

Two days after I had arrived in Ashcroft, Cecil had knocked on my door and invited me over to have coffee. Now, as I helped him clear out his unit, we talked again, about picking fruit in Washington State, about Texas, about California, about Alberta and about how the cowboys there were often racist assholes, and in that respect not too different from the cowboys in BC. Then we sat in the chairs outside his door on the ground floor, looking at the saddle and can of grease that lay on the wet strip of grass in front of us.

After a while Cecil said: "I grew up in a series of homes in Whitehorse. Did I tell you that?"

"No."

"I was brutalized as a boy. My stepdad used to punch me so hard that whenever I was around him I'd shiver and tremble. So as soon as I could I left. I first tried to leave when I was eleven."

He fell silent. Then he said, "Interesting. All that when I was a boy, it doesn't bother me now. The memories don't hurt."

"Something's bothering you," I said.

"How do you know?" He looked at me. "You think you know about me?"

"I don't think I know about you, Cecil. But I know something's bothering you."

He kept looking at me; then he looked out at the lot. After a while he said: "Yesterday, out at the Husky there at Cache Creek. Some guy calls me chief. I wanted to punch him. I wanted to punch him in the face."

"That's not so good."

"No it's not."

He looked down. And when he lifted his head again I saw it all in his face. "I wish I could change all this. It's my life problem. This stress. It won't let up. All the things I wanted to do when I was a kid, I didn't do 'em. The years went by and I just couldn't get out there, eh."

We sat in silence for a bit. Then I said, "You think you'll come back?"

"I don't know. Maybe. Probably. Yeah, I'll be back. If you come back to Ashcroft again, you'll see me around. We'll talk some more. I'm just restless. And listen —" He put his hand on my arm. "There's a guy you should talk to. His name is Les Edmonds. He used to be chief of the Ashcroft Band. Hell of a good man. He'll tell you things you should know. Okay?"

"Okay."

"All right." He stood up. "I gotta go. If I just stay here talkin' to you I might never leave."

I stood up with him and we shook hands. "Okay, Cecil. I hope you have a good trip. Good luck to you."

"You too. Oh, hey, one more thing. What about that Indian woman come around looking for you yesterday?"

"What Indian woman?"

"She said her name was Violet. She said she'd meet you at Frankie's at one this afternoon. You make fast time man."

"Well, that's me."

"That's you."

11

I was on my third cup of coffee and getting ready to leave when she finally rushed in. I stared at her, almost shocked. The last time I'd seen Violet she had looked fragile. Now she looked lean and alert, her small head framed by huge earrings shaped like dream catchers, and her face framed by a modified Mohawk, shaved at the sides and back, with a plume of hair on top and hanging down the nape of her neck in a style that emphasized her neck and cheekbones and gave her something of the magnificence of Wes Studi in the movie *Geronimo*.

But she was late; and that instability I remembered. Up at the reserve where she worked as the Native liaison to the elementary school, she had talked about auras, and I'd been surprised that she had the job she had. Still, as we talked I saw that she was tough and practical, and at times she made me laugh. "Sometimes I stick my foot in my mouth. Probably in terms of how I look the older people are definitely — well. The boys are more into it: 'That's cool.' But the girls are — 'Ooh, I can't figure that one out.' Maybe they're threatened by it. Young girls are so weird that way — everything threatens them. If I looked like an old mamma with long hair —"

"Tell me about that — the old mamma."

"The old Indian woman — they had to have long hair and all of it the same length. But I wanted to have a new look. And one day I just did it: I shaved my head here and back here, and that was it!"

"It looks terrific," I said.

"Thank you." She smiled and sipped her coffee.

A lot of the parents had been in residential schools. They had no idea how to be nurturing parents. And the community was small — pitifully small, maybe twenty-five adults. I started to see how the smallness of a reserve could work against it. "There's probably about nine mothers. My brother lives by himself, another brother lives by himself. Myself, May, Josie — we're single mothers. Of the married men they do have, some of the drinking is really bad. They say they don't drink, but they do.

"I have an uncle up there, George, everyone likes to hang around with George. He's the chief, he drinks all the time. I think if he ever sobered up he'd go really far. He's a natural artist. He's a really neat person. He's a really bright guy, but he suffered."

"How so?"

"We'd have to go down to the jail to get our dad's dad out of jail. We'd go without food and have to ask people for food." She smiled and leaned back. She sipped her coffee, then looked at me, still smiling. "I don't see him as our fearless leader."

As a child she had lived with George's mom and dad, her grandparents. "My grandfather played fiddle; he loved music, he'd bring the bar home with him. If you were up you got whipped. One time he was going to kill us. My grandfather was chasing us through the sagebrush with a rifle. He could see our shadows. So George got the bright idea of us ducking down."

I could see it: the two children running through the sagebrush on the hills above the river, the moon shining and giving them shadows. And visualizing this, thinking of the boy and girl on the run from an adult who was out to kill them, I saw for the first time the distance that separated my life experience from that of the Natives whom I had come to Ashcroft to talk to.

But I didn't feel oppressed. It was as if the beauty and silence of the little town transformed everything. Violet and George lying on the ground in the moonlight — the image struck me like something in a fairy tale, so that I could think about it and turn it over in my mind.

And again and again, talking to Natives in the days to come, I would have the same experience. Each time, as if I was seeing it through the wrong end of a telescope, something that normally would seem to me huge and terrible appeared ordinary and small. I would have to compensate afterward, making an imaginative effort — I would have to work hard to give the story its real dimensions and weight of grief, and often I didn't succeed.

12

Darlene, who was a friend of Wayne's and part Native and who would become one of my guides to Ashcroft, said to me one evening: "You want to go for a drive?"

We headed out in her Ford Ranger past ranches and old buildings, down dirt roads, then across the river towards the slough. All day it had been hot, the sky like a grey mattress on the mesas. Now the wind was blowing hard. Dust, small twigs and bits of cottonwood flew in the air. Black clouds filled the sky in the north and east, while in the west the sun shone, bathing the landscape in a lurid, underwater light. Across the river a train was going by. Because of the mesa's colour in the hallucinatory light, the train seemed to be floating in a straight line in the air.

And then the rain started. Within a minute it was whitening the air. Forks of lightning lit up the hills. A hundred yards in front of us lightning flashed down with an enormous sound and a tall tree burst into flames. I grinned. I rolled the window down a bit to smell the ozone in the wet air; the rain instantly wet my arm and my side of the seat. I rolled the window back up.

Darlene smiled nervously. "We shouldn't be out here in the lightning."

"Maybe so. But this is great."

We drove slowly along the river. And then, as suddenly as it had started, the rain stopped. All at once the world was silent. The hills had turned dark. The trees dripped. We drove through the wet, quiet town, then went up the Highland Valley road and stopped at the cut and got out.

I could smell sage in the chilly air. The cold wind blew in our faces. We climbed through a fence and walked to the edge of the cliff. I stared at the immense sandy stones of the mesa cut and the landscape beyond.

"Well, this is something," I said.

We could see fifty kilometres. The clouds hung below us like smoke, and in that smoke, stepped out from the canyon in layered sheets, mesas and hills extended into the distance, layer after layer of grey and green velvet, the darker, nearer hills black with trees and obscured by the smoke of clouds, then paling to blue and faintest blue and disappearing at the rim of the earth.

Darlene stood still, contemplating her world. Then she turned to me and smiled. "How'd you like to meet my friend Jeannette?"

13

We drove back through the silent town, then across the river and up the road to the reserve. Twilight now. Two satellite dishes. The houses on the reserve were spaced far apart on the great plateau. The wet hills rose dark at the plateau's rim, seeming weightless and far away. I felt the grandeur of the setting; the loneliness; the silence, except for the truck; the night coming on.

At Jeannette's house, a little dog barked at us. Then Jeannette herself came out, short, soft-voiced, clearly Native, talking almost in a whisper because it was late.

"So you're Bruce," she said, her voice kind and warm.

"I am he." I felt nervous.

"We've been hearing about you."

"Could we talk to you for a bit?" Darlene asked. She looked at me. "Would you like to have a coffee?"

"Sure. Of course."

"Otherwise we wouldn't be being polite."

"Well, we should be polite."

We went inside. Dark wood furniture; femininity; ruffled curtains; an abundance of things; a comfortable, neat clutter of objects. It was Jeannette's place. She said, "You should meet my husband," and led me into the living room.

He was sprawled on the couch, a white man with a rough face, bitter-looking. He wore jeans and a cowboy shirt. Jeannette introduced me. He didn't speak. I held out my hand. He looked at me, then he shook it. Then he went back to watching TV.

We drank coffee in the kitchen. It was that slightly weak coffee that people who drink a lot of coffee make.

After the storm, everything felt hushed. Jeannette told Darlene she would maybe have to quit managing the old folks' home in Ashcroft. She sounded worried. Her voice was soft. She said, "I'm feeling the stress. I've been getting migraines."

Stress. Cecil had used that same word. And as I listened to Jeannette and Darlene, I felt what I had also felt listening to Cecil: that difficulties were being relieved by talking about them quietly. It was something I would feel often later, talking with Natives — that sense of terrific stress under the quietness.

14

On a hot, windy Saturday, with dark clouds overhead and the sun on the dry clay roadside as white as the blast from a bomb, I once more drove out to Jeannette's place. She told me about her mom being murdered in a hotel in Vancouver. She said that other Natives had done it, Natives from another band. She had been five when it happened. She and her little brother had been in a locked room across the hall from her mom's room. Then she told me about going to residential school as a child and afterward living with a white family. For a while we sat side by side on her porch thinking and looking out across the reserve. Then Jeannette said, "You know, I've only recently moved back."

"Oh yeah?"

"Yeah. Ninety percent of my friends have been Caucasian. This is the first time in my life that I've really come back. It's still frightening. When I left here as a young girl I was thirteen. My aunt was doing a lot of drinking. She was half Irish and half Indian, you know, and when you get that full of beans you've got a devil on your hands."

Jeannette pointed to the little log church that stood by the reserve's graveyard. "I used to go and hide in the church all the time."

"Because of her drinking?"

"Yeah. She's an awful drinker. She got drunk and I'd be at home with the kids — you know, she had a couple little babies, they were beautiful little boys."

Jeannette sighed and leaned forward. "She got drunk one night and rolled on one little boy. He died. I was just thirteen and of course they wouldn't let me talk. I didn't know what had happened at first, then I found out that the baby had suffocated. There's a lot of pain."

"So you were getting away from a variety of things."

"Oh yeah."

15

We talked about prejudice; and then her thoughts took a turn that surprised me. "You know, when people haven't done things that are worth respecting people aren't going to give it to them. Most people have to earn that. And when you have a lot of people who don't want to get up to go to work in the morning —"

She stopped and looked at me. "They get a half a million dollars every three or four months, every three or four months of the year, and it's spread out to a certain family — well, I don't know. They don't work, they don't even go off to work anywhere."

I said, "Why is that?"

"It's politics, eh."

"You mean band politics?"

"Yes. Yes."

"How does it work?"

"Well, the government here gives each band so much money eh, to run their band offices and to look after the people. So welfare comes very easy. Like the housing thing. You get most of it paid for. I don't believe in that. I don't believe in taking handouts. I can see if you really need it, you've got a couple of kids, but I think, 'Get up and go to work like everybody else.' I don't believe in this equality thing."

I didn't know what Jeannette meant by that. But then, looking around at the similar houses of the reserve spaced far apart under the black clouds and blinding white sun, I thought maybe she meant everybody in the band being at an equal income level and on welfare and subsidized housing, unable to own their own homes. She said, "Everybody here knows how I feel and everybody in Ashcroft knows how I feel. I say, 'If you want respect, you have to earn that. You have to get out and show everybody else that you're just like them — hey, you're out there, you're earning, you're not just taking and taking and taking.'

"These handouts, I think they're one of the reasons why we've got a lot of people that aren't working. The Cache Creek ginseng farmers, they brought all these East Indians up here and gave them room and board in the hotel, they're giving them eight bucks an hour and yet all these people are on welfare here and they won't go out there to work? There is something wrong. You know, they have their priorities in the wrong place. They should put me in the government."

She smiled. And I realized that Jeannette's voice was now much stronger than it had been when she'd been talking about her childhood.

16

The black clouds were gone. The sky was blue from horizon to horizon and I could see a boy riding a horse towards us down a dirt road, each of the horse's prancing steps sending up a puff of dust in the sun.

"It's become a beautiful day," I said.

"Yeah." Jeannette looked around and lifted a hand. "Hello Jerz," she called out to the boy.

But her mind was elsewhere. "It's bad here. The morality is bad. A lot of the people here, all they do is drink or do drugs. We have child molesters here, and they shouldn't be allowed to live here but because it's one family they overlook it. You know, you can't just say, 'Well, just sweep it under the carpet, sweep the crimes and corruption under the carpet.' It's gotten so bad that I don't even have anything to do with half of our band because of it."

I said, "So there's actual corruption in how the money is distributed?"

"You bet," Jeannette said. "And I don't say that lightly. I say that in honesty. And everybody here knows how I feel. And the Indian chiefs know how I feel. I went down to Lytton — there was gonna be sixteen Indian chiefs down there — so I went down there to see what the chiefs thought. They have it all down on video. I got up and I told the whole works that —" she turned and looked straight at me, leaning forward, her voice suddenly fierce: "You know, they all talk about equality this and equality that, about being Indian, yet they never look themselves in the mirror. Well, half of them are white. I told them, 'You show me those bloody Indians, I'll show you a blonde and a blue-eyed one.' I told them, 'When you look down on the white people you're looking down on yourselves and you're looking down on your wife or your husband, you're looking down on your grand-children. My two little grandsons there, well they got Scotch in them, you know, and you're looking down on them when you say

only Indians are allowed to come back, with the Bill C-31 thing
—'"

"To come back to the reserve —"

"Yeah. Ah, the double standards in life, it's kind of upsetting
sometimes. I shouldn't even be talking about this. I, I get wound
up ha ha ha ha."

17

Whenever her emotions became intense, Jeannette laughed. It
was something new to me. The laughter let her skitter across
her pain like a skater on ice. Later I would see that Natives often
laughed this way. Laughter eased things; it lightened fear and
unease. It could be used in many ways. An Ashcroft journalist said: "We were up at Williams Lake at an editorial confer-
ence and we had the chief of the Alkali Lake band and one of
the negotiators for the province and one of the negotiators for
the federal government there. And when the Alkali Lake chief
spoke, he was very witty and pissed me off 'cause he had the typical Indian attitude: it was all funny to him, the whole goddamn
thing was funny."

Only with time did I come to see the damage this sense of
"funny" denoted.

18

As the weeks passed, I started to hear more about Leslie
Edmonds, the person Cecil had told me to see. "You want to
know about the reserve? He's the guy you should talk to."

And a little later: "Les, yeah. He used to be chief up there. He's
a wonderful man."

The praise made me dubious. But from the start Leslie – small,
handsome, one of those rare men in whom you could see the boy
he had been – from the start Leslie impressed me. As he spoke
that first day about his past — running away at fourteen from
the Lytton School to work on George Evans's potato farm in

Soda Creek, hitching down from Clinton and running up the side of the bank when he saw a car that might be a cop, working in Washington State at fifteen picking strawberries for Mr. and Mrs. Ellis ("They really treated me good. Didn't matter to them if I was a white little boy or an Indian little boy"), working at Empire Valley and in Revelstoke, and with each job learning more — more and more as we talked, I sensed in Leslie a person who was deeply connected to the part on the planet in which each of his small and large triumphs had occurred.

How clearly I could see the teenager and even the child in him! Each was there, available to Leslie, visible in his words. All his life, I thought, people will be attracted to him because of this.

Not that he'd been a stay-at-home. He had travelled: like most of the Natives I would talk to who seemed to me to be the least wounded or damaged, Leslie had left the reserve and then come back. But he remained a man of the Interior. And he represented the Interior to me.

19

"Finish your coffee," he said two days after our first meeting, sitting with me in the trailer in the Ashcroft Reserve where he and his wife Ruth ran a Native gift shop. "Take your time. Then we'll start." I removed my cap and he smiled slightly and raised his eyebrows, still amused at my white hair which, when I had taken off my *Ashcroft Journal* cap the first day, had made both him and Ruth smile. His own hair — as I could see now that he wasn't wearing a cap himself — was black, glossy, complementing his dark eyes and fine cheekbones, so that Leslie made me think of a Mongol warrior, a horseman from another time.

"Okay." I drank it, then looked at him. "So where were you born?"

"I guess I was born here in Ashcroft and I lived here all my life. I was about three months old when my mother got murdered in Vancouver."

"Murdered?" Like Jeannette's mom!

"Yeah. Her name was Jane Edmonds. I could never find any picture of her. To this day, after 52 years, I don't know what she looked like."

"What about your dad?"

"I never knew who my father was. The people that raised me was Willie Dyck. Willie Dyck was a spiritual healer."

"Were you brought up at all as a Christian?"

"No. Not till I was brought to the Lytton St. George's residential school."

"Tell me about that."

"Okay. I guess I was almost eleven years old when the RCMP arrived at our doorstep one day. Old Willie he went out to see what was the matter. I followed behind, I guess I was wanting to see. The RCMP asked, 'Is he Leslie Dyck?'"

"The old man responded to the RCMP this way." Leslie stuck his middle finger up. "The cop he just jumped out of his vehicle, grabbed me by the arm and threw me in. I didn't have time to say goodbye, didn't have time to change my clothes. We just left from there down to Lytton to the residential school. I cried all the way there. I didn't know what was happening. The cop wouldn't talk to me."

Leslie paused, letting me write. "A grey-haired old lady standing at the top of the stairs was waiting for me. Her name was Mrs. Joblin. I never knew what other names she had. That's all I ever knew. She took me from there, brought me up to the dormitory, scrubbed me down. They cut my hair real short, it was almost bald."

He moved a hand over his head, demonstrating. "I guess I just had to go mingle with the rest of the boys. In the basement there was a kind of a hole under the stairway. I crawled in there and I cried and cried and cried."

As he talked — talking calmly, choosing his words, sometimes briefly smiling — he rarely looked at me. Instead he looked out the window, inviting me by example to look with him, as if the world out there was a partner in our conversation.

He said: "Little lady her name was Miss Brandon. I couldn't remember how many pointers and yardsticks I used to see her breaking over these kids' faces and heads. Just because these kids couldn't speak English. She'd start whaling on them. Nobody was allowed to speak their own language. If you were caught you'd get strapped. You'd get punished. You'd go all day without eating.

"That's how we learned how to steal. We'd sneak down the fire escape, sneak into the kitchen or the garden behind the church. We'd sneak carrots or potatoes. Turnips. We'd get back upstairs under our covers and start chewing away. It sounded like a rabbit pen up there."

Leslie waited for me to catch up. "My number was 837. I'll never forget it. I sometimes use it in my 6-49 picks. There's this one particular guy who was number 838 that I got to be pretty good friends with. That kid, I don't think there was a day went by he didn't get a lickin'. Or very few. His name was Gilford Williams. Especially Miss Brandon used to get a joy out of beating him. Speaking his own language was a no-no. But he couldn't speak no other.

"This Gilford, he was about my age I guess. No matter how much he got licked, he wouldn't cry. His face would get beet red, mucus would come out of his nose but he just wouldn't cry. It got so bad one day that Miss Brandon broke down herself, she couldn't make Gilford cry.

"It got so bad that Gilford started peeing, wetting his bed every day eh? And every morning you could expect he'd be getting a lickin'.

"In the mornings about 4 or 5 o'clock he'd wake me up. He'd wake me up and whisper, 'Come give me a hand.' He'd wake up and wash his sheets in a toilet bowl. He'd want me to give him a hand wringing them out. He'd dry those sheets out on the radiator eh, before the matron'd come and wake us up. Before the matron would come in these sheets wouldn't be dry yet but he'd put them on his bed and cover them up with the blanket.

"And that's the first thing they'd do. They'd make him pull his blankets back and feel if the sheets were wet or damp. Strap."

20

I wrote in my notebook. Leslie waited. Then he said, "Come on. Let's go outside and have a smoke."

Out in the sun we sat on rounds of log and looked at the dirt road that led from the store out to the highway. A fox sat some distance away in the bunchgrass looking at us.

Smoking my cigarette, I studied its alert small body, its triangular face and big ears.

"I think this is the fox I saw a couple of days ago," Leslie said. "Might have to shoot it."

"Not while I'm here."

"You don't want me to?" Leslie smiled at me. "Don't worry. I won't shoot it while you're here."

Some customers drove up in an old dusty car — a young Native woman and her daughter. The daughter had a slack face, eyes oddly set; I guessed she had fetal alcohol syndrome. A little later Ruth walked out of the store holding a bill. "Les, you got change for a fifty?"

"Nope."

"What about you, Bruce?"

"No, I'm sorry."

She pursed her lips. "Guess they'll have to go down to town to get change."

Leslie gave a quick shrug — a flinch: it spoke of anxiety. And for the first time a tremor ran through the image I had of him.

21

Ruth brought us out another cup of coffee. While we were drinking it, Leslie lifted his chin towards the highway. "You see that motoplex up there?"

I looked where he meant, squinting in the sun. "I see it, yeah. The Ashcroft Band runs it eh? It's a dragstrip?"

"Yeah, well I started it. Around '78, '77, I'd done a lot of travelling down through the States looking at race tracks, dragstrips. I started getting a feel for a race track here. I started talking to a lot of people. So when the aeroclub that used to be in there finally pulled out I got into gear."

Leslie crossed his legs and leaned forward, an arm in his lap and the other upraised arm holding a cigarette. "It took me six years altogether. The hardest part was dealing with the bureaucrats. I spent many days and many miles going back and forth to Vancouver. They'd never heard of Ashcroft. Some of their questions were so stupid that I really couldn't answer them.

"Anyway, when we finally got the thing going, everybody in the area was so happy about it. The Ashcroft Ranch helped out with their machinery. Then we had a whole bunch of people that worked on the mines — they'd get off shift and get on their machinery and get it levelled out. People just all jumped in with both feet and supported me.

"But you know, when I asked my band members for help none of them helped me. It was really discouraging for me. But I just kept on going."

Leslie smoked. "I only got four years of education. A lot of the material I'd read I couldn't understand. So I'd have to hunt around for somebody I could trust would set me straight on it."

He looked at me. "That's how I do things. I've got a lot of good friends both in the Native and white communities that I can trust. If I've got a letter I take it to them and show it."

I said, "Do you get along with George Kirkpatrick?"

"Our current chief? Yeah, I get along with him. But over the years I've learned not to trust him too far. What he says with one hand and what he does with the other are two different things. He's chief and his brother's the councillor. They get all the good jobs."

Leslie considered, looking out into the afternoon. "That particular family is in power now and they use welfare in their campaign. And they get people drunk. They scare people that I'm gonna cut them off welfare."

I looked out side by side with him and thought about what Jeannette had told me. After a moment I said, "So there's nepotism in the band."

"Nepotism. What's that?"

"That's when somebody hires somebody who's in their family for a public position. It's a bad thing."

"Nepotism, eh. That's a damn good word." He smoked. And it was as if he was turning the word over in the air and considering it. "Yeah, well we got it here. When I was chief I built five houses, I drilled a well, I put a pipeline in all the way up to the racetrack. In three months!

"And those houses that were built when I was in office were the only ones that were ever paid for honestly. The rest of the houses aren't paid for. People don't pay, even when they have pockets full of money. Because they can't collect. They can't kick us out.

"I think that the whole structure of the reserves should change," Leslie said. "It wouldn't change overnight. But I think it should change."

He smoked. "Way back when, when I was first elected chief, I involved myself in a joint venture with Foothills Pipeline. We done a pipeline job in Hope. I got five band members involved in the union. But as soon as the job was over, they didn't keep up their union dues, so all my efforts dried on the vine. That is one of the . . . "

He put out his cigarette in the ashtray by his foot and lit up another. His eyes closed under his cap. And at that moment, the feeling I had had since I'd met him of Leslie being grounded, rooted in a place, gave way to an almost terrifying sense of fragility. It was as if the earth had opened beneath us. The link to the past that had seemed so strong in him — that had made him attractive to me, glamorous, allowing him at any moment, I thought, to resurrect the boy he had been, the link that had let him see everything that had happened in his life as part of the old slow course of the world — now I realized that that link had long since been broken.

After a while he said, "Since I haven't been a chief everything's been at a standstill. Like the graveyard. Because they didn't have the money to hire somebody to clean it up, they didn't clean it up. So before Easter I came in with a few people, then a few people more. We repaired the crosses, fixed the fences. And then it was held against me."

I said, "Have you thought about running for chief again?"

"Maybe some time. But now ... my nerves have been bothering me."

Nerves! I remembered Jeannette, speaking hesitantly to Darlene about how she might not be able to go to work because of her migraine; and I remembered Cecil telling me about his fear of going out into the world.

"I don't know," Leslie said after a moment. "I guess maybe it's not the right time." And then he laughed and there it was again, that thing that let Natives skate across their grief, that let them at least temporarily turn shame, humiliation and anger into light things, trivialities, part of the everyday, nothing to get upset about.

The Light on the Tracks
Part Two

1

For weeks it had been hot, with a heat I hadn't known before. Sometimes it rained at night and big puddles formed in the parking lot, but by morning the puddles had evaporated and all you could see were concentric yellow rings of pollen like the rings around an alkali lake. When people stepped out of their units after breakfast you'd see them squeeze their eyes shut and stand still with the sun on their faces like masks of gold. The heat stung my skin: even before 9 AM the thermometer by my door sometimes read 30 degrees.

Then the weather changed. And one Saturday morning when I stepped outside a cold wind was blowing tumbleweeds against the parked cars. The wind on my face decided me. The day before I'd seen a poster in the Ashcroft Radio Shack advertising a gathering of Seventh Day Adventists in Lillooet; now, responding to that poster, I washed my breakfast dishes and packed up the van.

I had heard from Wayne (and pretty much everybody else I'd talked to in Ashcroft, including Ray and Max) that people in the Interior weren't like people in Vancouver. They didn't stay stuck in one neighbourhood. Typically they had an area of about five hundred kilometres that they felt at home in. They drove the country roads ("Ray drives me," Max said), they fished, they camped, they hunted. That country was theirs.

Hearing this, I had decided – in order to get a sense of what it felt like to have such a huge home area – to go out to the Anahim Lake Stampede, which took place in the far west Chilcotin. My first stop, though, would be the Seventh Day Adventist Gathering in Lillooet.

Wayne, Ray, Max were sitting in chairs on the walkway, all three with jackets on. Wayne waved as I backed out of the lot, and I lifted my hand in return.

2

I had been in Lillooet before, when I'd first come into the BC Interior and decided to write about it. Now once again I found a spot at the Cayoosh Campground down near the Fraser. And once again, after I had boiled water and made a cup of instant coffee, I walked around the site, exploring it now with the attentiveness that comes with familiarity.

Dry dirt, so dry it turned to dust between your fingers; bushes, some of them hay-yellow; nearly dead grass; a few trees; a white gravel path sketching out the road for cars. Further towards the river the campground's owners were grading in an attempt to improve the place. Their work gave the site what I would later think of as the look of a prairie farm: a strip of bare dirt, then bushes, then the river.

The river at my front, the rising cut of the highway at my back. A rough place — like Lillooet itself, I could see now. As I had, most of the campers had nestled between the bushes, as much out of the wind as possible.

I realized now that Lillooet had grown up at the intersection of two deep valleys. That day the valley that went west to the coast was lit up by the afternoon sun and seemed like an entrance to the edge of the world. Our own austere, windy campsite was set in the other valley, which was almost a canyon — a rock face of cliffs rose up right in front of me, made dark by the near-black rain clouds that I could see when I looked straight up, even while the sun shone hot on my neck.

And then, as I walked towards the river, deja vu swept over me. A woman was shouting from a huge recreational vehicle: "Quit doing that! I told you you've got work to do! Andrew, stop playing around in that ash, you're gonna get filthy!"

Listening to this woman whose every word I had heard before, my deja vu deepened so that the hairs stood up on my neck. A logging truck had pulled in, carrying two lo-bed trailers loaded with logs — poles really, no more than three inches across. I had seen those loads of sticks before. But where?

The driver got out of his truck. I shuddered looking at him. At each moment I knew what he was going to do next. As if I was watching an old film, I saw his attention shift from the inside of his cab to the ground to me. The sunlight picked out his small eyes. He was a man in his thirties, wearing a cap and jeans but no shirt. An immense stomach. He lifted up his arm and sniffed under his armpit.

"What's goin' on up there?" he called out.

"Seventh Day Adventists."

He walked over to me and together we walked to the edge of the campsite. A big white tent had been set up for the night's meeting. The sign near the tent — a sign like the kind found at gas stations — said: "The Mark of Satan / The Seal of God." Off to the side in the blowing dirt stood military-style half-barrel tents.

The meeting was at eight. I looked at my watch: 5:45.

"Well, there's still time," I said.

"Time for what?" The truck driver stared at me, his close-set eyes so small and empty of feeling they looked like the eyes of a bear. He wandered off down the road. I watched him go, feeling sadness and fear. It was turning cold. The sun shone on the canyon wall, but where I stood it was evening. I shivered and went back to my campsite and tried to cheer myself up making a hot supper of beans and wieners and broccoli. I read, but got little solace from my book. At around quarter to eight I set out.

3

Dark now, the blowing wind very cold. It hurt my face and it hurt my knees through my pant legs. I walked in the dark across rutted dirt that crumbled beneath my shoes. With each step, the wind lifted dust. In front of me a young Native man wearing black jeans and a black Western shirt was holding his cowboy hat down with one hand. Also moving slowly towards the tent was an older couple walking in from their camper, each of them carrying a Bible and looking in that darkness like gloomy penitents.

What had I expected? Not what I found. Clean white sawdust on the floor. White plastic chairs lined up in neat rows under two strings of light bulbs. Plants hanging near the front, close to an electric organ, and big pictures of heaven and hell, bright as comic-book covers, on stands. Best of all, even while the cold wind rattled the tent's heavy zipper and made the strings of lights shake, here in the tent it felt warm. A stern man standing a few feet in from the entrance greeted people he knew, putting his arm around the older couples, murmuring a few words to the family groups. I saw some teenagers, three or four cowboy hats.

"Hello! Is Jesus with you tonight?"

I straightened up. "Well, I'm not sure."

The girl's face was as cheerful and bright as her words. She was seated behind a folding table covered with stacks of "Revelation" books and a series of pamphlets I had been examining.

She smiled. "All right."

I didn't want to mislead her. "The truth is, I'm just visiting. I'm camping — and I was curious about the meeting."

"That's okay. We've gotten a lot of people who are just curious. Everyone's welcome. Tonight's a bit heavy, though."

I picked up a couple of the pamphlets and then sat at the edge of a row near the back so I could make my exit quietly.

A little girl sat next to me, staring forward, wide-eyed. Her small hands were folded politely in her lap. What was she thinking? Of God, perhaps; of how interesting these adults looked, seated in their formal best; of how pious and good she herself must look. I remembered it all; and for a moment I was back in the basement of Hinton's Athabaska Hotel, where before the church had been built the town's Catholics had celebrated mass. Then, too, strings of lights had hung from the ceiling, strange people had come in from the night's surrounding dark.

But the Catholic priest had had the authority of his church. And I had still believed. The man who now got up to speak wore a suit and had a blonde pompadour. His face was tight, hectic. And immediately I thought: He's terrible. He talks too fast, the smile in his voice reeks of desperation. He said: "Here we are on this beautiful blustery night! Nice to be out of the wind eh? You bet it is!"

Even while he spoke, stumbling in his desperation over his trivial material, people kept coming in. The regulars were greeted, commiserated with. An old lady on crutches. A raw-boned couple.

The man with the pompadour was unable to sweep away the mild disorder. Finally he sat down. The Native man who had walked in ahead of me got up and faced the gathering. "Well," he said, "I hope you had an easy time comin' — comin' here. We're gonna have a good night, I think. We're gonna talk about the charactistics — the charac — the charactiss —"

He stopped. He grinned. "Sorry about that," he said. "I'm an Indian and us Indians don't speak English so good."

Someone groaned.

The Native man sat back down. The man with the pompadour stood up again. In a loud voice he said: "What is the mark of the beast?"

Half the crowd shouted: "Worshipping on Sunday!"

This was the mark of their religion, the distinguishing trait — that they worshipped on Saturday instead of Sunday. The rest of the Christian church had been misled by Papacy! They had all gone astray!

At that moment I felt for the first time what a few years later I would see as one of the most unexpected features of a trip I took across the prairies (I would travel as far east as Pine Falls, Manitoba): the extent to which religion and faith and virtue — older words, hardly used by the people I knew in Vancouver — the extent to which these words continued to mean something for people in the country, the extent to which the faces around me had been shaped by ideas and ways of feeling connoted by those words. For the first time I felt that a way of being in the world which I associated with a much earlier time continued to exist in the west, especially in places where the great basic shapes of the land still formed people's lives. For the first but not the last time I sat with a group of people who defined themselves by sectarianism in its oldest form.

"What are the four most important things?" the man with the pompadour said.

A long silence. Then a man in the audience said, "To be born."

"Amen. And what else?"

"To be born again."

"That's right. And what else. They're the simplest things! They're like falling off a log! That's how God intends it!"

"To be married and to die! Amen, Lord!" an old woman sang out.

"Amen! That's it! The four most important things are: to be born, to be born again, to marry, and to die. You *need* to be born again because we all are born with original sin."

The man rubbed his hands. "Now I'm gonna ask for questions from the audience. Don't be shy now."

The man who had first spoken — a young broad-shouldered man holding a baby — asked, "Why did people change the Sabbath to Sunday?"

"Let me tell you, the *pope* isn't the leader; the papal church says the whole world worships us. They changed the day of worship from Saturday to Sunday."

"Why do you only use the King James Bible?" a woman asked.

"The New World translation was done by Jehovah's Witness scholars — over three thousand changes. Let me tell you. Peter is not the rock; Petros in Greek means little pebble; petra means rock. *Jesus* is the rock. Peter, you're the devil himself!"

A thin older man quoted Deuteronomy. When he finished, his finger still in his Bible, he said, "What I'm sayin' is, I'm askin', why do we allow women to wear these unisex clothes?"

The man with the pompadour smiled at him. "I hear where you're comin' from. But you know, I've heard some say, a woman shouldn't wear pants today, but obviously a woman *can* wear pants and you can still tell she's a woman." He winked.

With that wink, the mood in the tent changed. People shook their heads. They wanted no jokes. They wanted harshness and to be wrapped tight in strictures. The congregation now seemed small and unsure of itself, oppressed by the darkness outside. Sensing this, the man with the pompadour said, "Now, let's do our children. We're gonna have a baptism here this Sabbath, that'll be really exciting."

"Wow," somebody said.

"And tomorrow, we're gonna talk about Bible health. God's been ahead of medical science for centuries. You'll love it, it'll be powerful, you don't want to miss it."

Two men passed out buckets for money; and while the buckets were being handed down the rows, the man with the pompadour started talking about God's wrath: "Two times in Biblical history God lets us really see his anger. The *first* time we see God's wrath was the time of the flood. God looked around at people and said, 'I'm *sick* of this; I'm sick of what I've done.' And out of an estimated two to three billion people he let only eight live. There were only eight righteous people on the earth at that time. The *other* time we see God's wrath was Sodom and Gomorrah."

The bucket had reached me. I put in three dollars and a bit of change, then got up and left.

4

That night in the van I opened the back doors and listened to the wind, the trucks on the highway, and then in the deep night, the sound of the sawmill. Once again I was awake at night in Lillooet. But I felt differently than I had before. I felt intent, fully alive. At 4 AM I went outside and stared up at a nearly full moon hanging above the canyon.

5

In the morning, after breakfast in town, and tired from my lack of sleep, I drove in the bright sun east on Highway 12. The coffee started to work: I enjoyed the folded hills, the canyons with their steep vertical shadows and bands of intense light rising up right by the road.

At Highway 97 I turned north.

Logging trucks on the highway; tractor-trailers hauling gasoline; Safeway and Overwaitea trucks; trucks carrying wood chips; recreational vehicles with BC and Alberta and Washington and Oregon and Montana and California licence plates; old farming trucks with haybales stacked up fifteen and twenty feet high that disintegrated in the highway airstream and strewed hay and dried grass over the asphalt.

At Clinton where I stopped for lunch and wrote notes, the sun on the white paper was so bright that when I looked up the world had turned dark. But then the weather changed. The wind picked up; the sky clouded over. The road became shadowless and darkness hung between the trees.

6

That evening as I drove out towards Brunsen Lake I passed two Native men standing on the side of the road. An older model Honda Civic had gone off the highway into the ditch. The two men were looking at it. They were bulky men with severe faces, dressed in dark clothes.

I stopped the car a bit up the road and got out. A month earlier I might have felt anxious speaking to the two men. Now, after my time in Ashcroft, having started to understand a little the world in which they lived, I was concerned; I wanted to hear what they had to say.

"What happened?"

"Car drove off."

"Is anybody hurt?"

"Nobody there."

"They walked off."

"This happens all the time."

"Kids. They don't know ..."

"Is there a campsite up ahead?"

"You can ask at the reserve."

7

It was starting to rain when I reached the Alkali Lake reserve. The sky was a muddy grey and the wind lifted the windshield wipers even when I stopped the car to look at the wooden statue of Jesus that stood at the reserve entrance.

Painted blood dripped from the statue. I recognized that blood: it expressed the Catholicism I had grown up with, so indelible with its images of tortured saints and unending hell. Not since I'd left Hinton had I seen my childhood religion depicted like this. Only in books, in pictures that came from old Europe, had I found anything similar.

I had enjoyed those pictures. But this statue — maybe because it was in the bush, in BC, a world I knew, with the raw sky overhead — this statue looked horrific. It suited the reserve, though, which that evening seemed to be situated at the end of the world.

I drove slowly up the reserve's gravel road. Over all that I passed hung a terrible, killing stillness that I recognized from other reserves I had gone through — the stillness of a place where people have absolutely nothing to do.

Each house had concrete steps — steps without rails, a block of cast concrete — going up to the raised front door. And just as I had recognized the blood on the statue, I recognized those steps. In Hinton, as a small child, I had played beside just such steps, steps in front of company houses, the concrete crumbling where it met the dirt, and in and among the bits of concrete and dirt, daddy longlegs, crawling in and out of webby holes.

At one of the houses a man was standing on the top step in front of the door. A boy was standing in the dirt yard below him. Both were looking at me. I went up to ask for directions.

"I hear there's a campsite out near Brunsen Lake. Do you know how to get to it?"

"No, I don't," the man said.

"Is there anyone around who could tell me?"

"No."

He wasn't being unfriendly; his face was a mask of grief. And for hours afterward, I could see him in my mind's eye, standing there on the porch of his house, the boy (maybe his son) in the muddy yard, the bush at his back, the rain falling and a few hundred yards away that statue by the gravel turnaround.

8

When I finally found the campsite I unpacked the van. The storm had been at my back all afternoon; now it caught up to me. With the wind and rain, the muddy sky quickly turned dark. And then I discovered a further darkness: the site had been fouled by cattle, with piles of dung on the bare ground and a filthy scum of excrement and dead plants and dead fish all along the edge of the lake.

That night in the van I lay in my sleeping bag staring up at the dark. Over the past two months I had become used to camping, used to spending nights in the van; but now the wind blowing the van's walls, the cold rain, the sounds of the cattle in the bush, the thought of their dung lying on the muddy ground outside and, each time I closed my eyes, the image of the man standing on the porch of his house and the blackness that had seemed to me to be all around him — all this came together in a sense of threat.

I strained to hear noises. I knew that in a place this run down (I had already seen beer cans and broken whiskey bottles on the edge of the bush) drunkards could come; and I thought that the young Native boys and girls, so on their own and angry, might have an all-night spree, something I had already experienced. I was out in the world, just as I'd been with my dad and my brother Mike in various motels in the US in earlier years; and just as I had then, I felt desolation: I could feel the site's wildness and indifference pressing against the van's walls.

9

That morning I woke to fog and mist. Sheets of vapour were rising off the lake. The trees were still black. A cold white light filled the air. Cattle were bunched up by a big ponderosa pine that rose by itself into the fog on a low hillside.

As I drank coffee and packed up the light brightened and brightened. The mist above the trees at the eastern end of the lake became translucent. And then a long wedge of blue sky appeared; and while I was shaking out bedding on the van's hood, the sun suddenly shone on the water droplets on the car and turned the spider webs clinging to the tall grasses into a brilliant dazzle.

With the sun up and the air clear, feeling happy, I drove to Williams Lake and then down onto Highway 20. A famous road, stretching across the Chilcotin all the way to Bella Coola. I had read about it often, but I'd never driven on it. And it surprised me. I didn't know that you had to go down and down to the Fraser River before you crossed the river, and that you then had to go up and up, up the side of a cliff, turning and turning as if on one of the mountain roads of my childhood. I hadn't expected this, the hard driving or the need to pay attention. I leaned forward, resigning myself; and then the sky yawned and I was on the plateau and all my driving difficulties fell away.

I almost stopped. So abrupt, the change! After the congestion of Highway 97 — the campers and trucks — the long straight empty road seemed dreamlike.

The sky amazed me. A 360-degree sky, like the sky on the

prairies, it contained rank after rank of clouds. They were anvil-shaped, flat on the bottom, the tops puffy and rising high; and the form of each exactly repeated the form of every other. With the clouds huge overhead and becoming smaller and smaller in the distance, this repetition of exactly the same form made the sky look like an hallucination. Off in the distance, thirty or forty kilometres away, bluffs. Once — like a faint print in the middle distance of the air — I got a glimpse of the Coast Range.

In Alexis Creek, at the Cook Shack across from the Chilcotin Hotel, I bought a butter tart for a dollar from the overweight proprietor. I asked about camping.

He pointed. "Six kilometres up the road. There's a big sign. You can't miss it. Bull Canyon."

10

A beautiful spot that day, full of light and shade. In the steep narrow valley the greenish-grey Chilcotin River flowed quickly, campers kept away from its strong current by a tightly made caribou fence. The campsite I chose was immersed in aspen leaves like medals, trembling and reflecting light all around me. The late afternoon air was sweet and crystal clear — the rock bluffs stood out behind me in the sun.

Driving through the Chilcotin I had felt happy. I'd been alert, concentrating on each moment, my thoughts rarely moving beyond the present. Now in the campsite, as I unpacked, that alert happiness stayed with me. Seed pods drifted through the afternoon sunlight; black ants walked up onto the picnic table; a shiny black beetle walked through the dirt; a squirrel climbed down a tree, looking for food. I stepped to the edge of my campsite and looked around, stretching my arms. A man wearing an expensive sweater draped over his shoulders walked past, his hands in his pockets. "Hi," I said; at the last possible moment, he glanced at me.

I suppose it was then, when I saw his unfriendliness, that I realized I was the only person in a van and also the only single person. And at that moment my delight in being there vanished. Among these rich tourists with their huge recreational vehicles, I was poor.

How easily dismay takes hold when you feel poor. I felt ashamed of my jeans and old van; I wanted to hide in the van. Making it worse, at the moment I realized that I wanted to hide, a heavyset man with a red face walked towards me, talking on a cell phone to some friends who were slowly driving their more-than-bus-sized recreational vehicle down into the park. I disapproved of the man's loud voice and red face; I disapproved of his cell phone and the way he paced importantly back and forth; but beneath my disapproval (the man was ignoring me: the disapproval meant nothing to him), anxiety flared in me. And I thought: This is how the Natives must often feel. The year before, driving into the Pemberton Valley, I had passed through a Native blockade. Men and boys and a couple of young women had sat on the side of the road outside a convenience store; a man had ridden by me on a bicycle; and in all their faces — the faces of people in jeans and without cars confronting people driving past in twenty- and thirty- and forty-thousand-dollar vehicles — in all their faces I had seen the same anxiety I felt now. How much humiliation, I'd thought as I drove past, lay behind their stiff, self-conscious movements as they walked towards the highway, their hunched shoulders and angry and uncertain eyes!

11

I read; I made supper. I tried to cheer myself up by thinking that I looked like a cowboy with my denim shirt and jeans. While I was stirring my soup, a young bloodhound came over, eager to make friends. It walked right up to me with its young dog's bouncing walk — jowls hanging, balls dangling behind — and put its paws on my leg and licked my hand. It had the same sad eyes as the actor William H. Macy.

"Good dog," I said.

It walked around the table. Then it caught a scent: it looked up the hill, then walked into the bush, occasionally stopping and sniffing.

About 8:30, the warden, a friendly woman, Native or part-Native with dark skin and black eyes and a gap in her teeth, talked with me about the Anahim Stampede.

"It's great. The cowboys are falling off their horses, but everyone's there to have fun. The Indians really like to have a good time. Don't stay overnight, though. They'll rob you blind."

Grateful in my loneliness to be talking to another human being, I asked, "What's your name?"

"Chris Robertson."

I held out my hand. "Pleased to meet you Chris."

The next day dawned hot and bright, with no clouds. I packed up and set off on Highway 20, the Chilcotin Road, for Anahim.

12

Near Redstone Reserve, the road running directly west, I saw the Coast mountains dead ahead. After that, the Chilcotin plains stretched out for thirty kilometres or more and were ringed by wooded bluffs that were as flat on top as mesas. It was a scene from a landscape in my dreams, those wooded bluffs rising up from the grasslands, and rising above the bluffs, printed in the air, the mountains.

After Tatla Lake the road turned to gravel. Dust, pebbles hitting the underside of the van, but at this time of year no real potholes. The road wound through wooded bluffs and along valleys.

And all at once, coming over a rise and seeing the road wind down below, a happy excitement filled me. What caused it at first was obscure. Only after a few minutes did I realize that the dusty bushes on the roadside, the light colours of the gravel and the gravel's texture had all spoken to me of the past. It was a road like the roads of Hinton. The lakes — and this added to the sense of happiness the scenery gave me, though again for a few minutes I didn't know why — the lakes were a brilliant deep blue like the lakes of northern Alberta; and like my childhood lakes they refreshed the eyes after the tans and whites of the road, the dull dark green of the conifers and the yellowish green of the grass.

At the Anahim Stampede grounds cars were lined up in rows in a field and parked every which way on the bank leading up to the lot. One 4X4 truck was parked almost straight up. Horses were tied up in a row at a long sun-bleached post fence. Some of the tethered horses had their saddles on them.

Kids were playing under the bleachers, and kids were crawling under the chickenwire fence surrounding the beer garden. They wanted to look at a drunk who was lying on his side with a big hearing aid in his ear. An old Indian woman with a walker sat on the ground, her legs straight out. I walked past groups of standing men, Native and white, all of them drinking, one of the white men with serious, staring, unfocused eyes, telling his story, quite drunk. All at once I realized that I had arrived at one of the last few frontier places in Canada.

Sitting in the sun in the old bleachers, Allison, the woman on my left, gulped her beer and said, "So. What brings you out here?"

"Oh, just looking."

"Where you from?"

"Vancouver."

"And you're out here just looking."

"Well, I heard about the stampede —"

She grinned at me. "Oh yeah, and what did you hear?"

"I heard it was a good time."

She laughed, a generous, sexual laugh that went with her black eyes and sunburnt face and her open-throated cowboy shirt that showed off her breasts. "You want a good time, you shoulda been line dancing at my mom's cabin last night. God, we had fun!" And then she laughed some more at a friend who walked up wearing a straw hat with the ends frayed and with the top ripped open.

"You look great! You look like a round hay bale!"

On the other side of me sat a man wearing two cowboy hats.

Snorting with laughter, snuffling, then wiping his nose, he passed his cup of beer to the man he was sitting with. This second man was older, with silver hair. He pointed to the little kids crawling under the chickenwire fence and called out to the Indian couple who were drinking below us:

"Hey Mary, you should keep your kids under control!"

"They're not my kids!"

The fence surrounding the beer garden part of the stands stood about five feet high. By now four kids had crawled under it where it had bellied out.

A man greeted his friend:

"Joseph!"

"How you doin', Bob!"

"Pretty good." Bob pointed to his wife: "I had to fasten my seatbelt. Quite a driver, boy. I had to slow her down."

She had driven them up from Bella Coola.

People were greeting each other almost constantly.

"Molly!"

"Oh Joan! You got your spring done?"

"Just about."

"Where you two sittin'?"

"How's the weather bin up at the lake?"

"Gettin' work?"

"Oh — a bit here, a bit there."

I saw: a foppish man with an orange bandana around his throat and false teeth slipping in his mouth. A Native man wearing a lime-green cowboy hat. A bearded bushman with staring eyes in his sunburnt face; and a biker couple from Ontario laughing with an older woman. As she laughed, the older woman let the straps of her tank top slide off her shoulders. One of her breasts slipped out. The biker looked at me and smiled: his two front teeth were missing.

People were talking about horses, laughing, joking.

"Bob could hardly stand up. And he had that twenty-two eh? And he's wavin' it, wavin' it around. And he says, 'Get out of here you miscreant.' And he shoots the bed. Shoots the bed."

13

I liked it all — the people talking, the kids playing. I liked the
sweaty faces, the happy, beery eyes, the boys and girls sitting on
the fences, the boys in bright shirts and the girls in tight jeans
and boots. I had a sense of something theatrical. Everyone here
knew each other. Each person had a history; and at this festive
event, those histories were being brought forward and retold.
And I liked the rodeo itself. It felt more relaxed and less macho
than other rodeos I'd been to. It was an amateur rodeo: the cowboys sitting by the chutes didn't turn away from the women's
events as they would have at a professional event. And I didn't
feel that metallic, hyper-masculine style that had made a few
rodeos I'd attended seem so sombre. Native women ran the concession; it was a Native event. And it had a Native feeling. People
seemed casual, inattentive; but when something good happened,
a horse bucking right up into the air, for instance, they whooped
and shouted.

A man was hammering part of the fence together. I could hear
the sound of his hammer as I walked towards the concession, and
something about that flat carpenter's sound there in the bright
sun with the trees around me and the smells of the concession
food made my heart beat a little faster.

The man stopped hammering. He stared at me; then he smiled
and raised his hammer. It was Cecil.

14

I felt almost unreasonably happy. I said, "What are you doing
here?"

"*Me?* What about you? At least I'm workin'. You just ride
around goin' to stampedes?"

He had to work: he was a volunteer. But we talked briefly. He
had a friend — a woman — who lived out near the Redstone
Reserve and he often spent time with her. "Especially now, since
I got the job working on the highway. Good pay, too."

A boy walked over. He knew Cecil: he had come here with Cecil's friend. He said he was twelve. He looked eight, under-nourished and melancholy and with black circles around his eyes.

"Where do you go to school?"

"Lytton."

"You like it?"

"Yeah." He worked on a farm.

"What's it like?"

"It irritates me. Got to herd for twelve hours."

He was vague about his parents. "My dad died. My name's Lyndon Bateman, but it was gonna be Walkem." Which was a big name around Lytton.

He guessed he lived with relatives. "I'm Indian. I live with the Cook's Ferry Band."

"You don't look Indian."

"My grandfather was part white and my mom."

He had a slight lisp. As he talked, he sometimes dropped gobs of white boyish spit on the ground, imitating the cowboys.

"What are you doing, taking pictures?"

"Yes."

"For a paper?"

"Not exactly."

We talked about that. I told him about the paper I edited.

"I know that paper — the *Review*," he said. "The *Vancouver Review*. You're a journalist?" He paused. "That's like an artist."

In the arena now a boy rode a steer right up to the whistle. His friends called out. But he was serious — he gave the steer a brush-off wave and went over to the bell-rope and tugged at it.

The boy had seen what I saw. He said: "Did you see that. His friends were waving to him, wanted to get his attention. But he had no time for them. Serious. He was after that rope. He's a *man*."

I thought of the enormous "No Snivelling" sign that hung on the back wall in Ashcroft's Drylands Arena.

15

I could have stayed and talked to Cecil. But I felt overwhelmed by all that had happened that day; I wanted to be alone. I asked Cecil to recommend a place for the night and he told me about a good campsite above Tatla Lake.

It clouded over a little after six. I threw my campground guidebook on the fire and watched it slowly burn. It expanded like a book puffing out in water but much more; the pages turned black, flat black like a widow's dress; they curled and twisted; and slowly, like a complicated black origami, the sleek, glossy-papered book turned into an intricate, thick, archaic-looking object.

Looking at the fire, I saw a tiny dust-coloured frog jump among the stones. I picked it up and brought it to the edge of the lake. When I put it down I saw a miniature green frog, an inch or so long, exactly the size of the dust-coloured frog. I thought: How extravagant nature is! I brought the little frog back and fell asleep thinking about coloured frogs and about making my way back to Ashcroft.

16

The little town seemed quiet after Highway 97. I drove slowly down Railway. Nothing was going on; no one was on the street. The drug store was closed. At the Ashcroft Motel, a man whom I knew only as Old Jack sat on the exercise bike outside his door staring at the railroad tracks. I looked with him, and even as we watched, the silver light pooled on the tracks drained away, leaving parallel strips of slag.

I parked and got out of the van. Dark clouds were gathering overhead, and I could hear a couple of voices carried by the wind; other than that it was absolutely still.

Then I saw Wayne: he was standing in the doorway of his unit. He caught my eye and walked quickly over and shook my hand. "Bruce! Boy, it's good to see you! I thought you'd gone already. I thought you'd gone home. I'm glad you're back."

He was almost in tears. I was life to him: possibility. I felt pathos. I would be leaving soon, and he would be staying on. Already he seemed to me to fade, to become ghostlike.

While I had supper the wind picked up. Dust clouds thirty feet high blew in the empty street. The clouds kept darkening. Finally I went outside onto the second floor walkway.

Ray and Max were leaning on the railing. I felt nervous seeing Ray. We had fought. Before I'd gone on my trip to Lillooet, we had made a date to go to the racetrack, where Ray worked as a volunteer. I'd become sick with giardiasis and unable to meet him. When I'd tried to explain myself to him the day after we had agreed to meet — I had called his name, seeing him walk towards me as I was talking to Sharon on the motel phone — he had walked by, not "seeing" me. I had been angered at that, wounded by the unforgiving pride.

But that had been more than a week ago. Now Ray smiled at me: "Hey, you talkin' to me? Come on over. Have a smoke."

I said, "Come on, Ray, you walked past me like I shitted on you."

"Well, you were talking on the phone to your wife. I didn't want to bother you. Come on, let's not fight. Have a cigarette."

I took the cigarette he held out. And then we leaned together on the railing, the three of us, Ray the small Native man between two whites, binding us together while we talked about the lightning Ray and Max both expected any moment now.

Max said, "Ions, that's what it is."

Ray said, "I love fucking lightning and thunder. It's better than sex."

Max said, "It lasts longer."

"Speak for yourself."

Clouds like black mould filled the sky. Lightning started to shine behind them above the hills and we heard a low grumble of thunder.

Ray said, "There's parts of the world where people think the gods are angry at them, lightning and thunder."

Max said, "You've been watching too much of that *Hercules*."

"No man! People are superstitious."

I said — glad to be talking to Ray again, and speaking out of this gladness — "He's been watching *Xena, Warrior Princess.* Ray's got the hots for those tits and thighs."

"Lucy Lawless, man."

Max said, laughing, "Could you imagine bein' her husband? 'I WANT IT NOW!' And that sword?"

Ray said, "I wouldn't mind bein' her husband for a while."

We saw our first lightning flash.

Ray started counting: "One ... two ..."

"No — you got to count one and a thousand, two and a thousand," Max said.

"I hope it's not a fake rain."

Lightning flashed right near the mesa — blinding white and then immediately a *CRACK!* And then the rain started; within a minute it was a monsoon. The air cooled and filled with the smells of wet sage and wetted dust. We smiled, feeling the cool, perfumed air on our faces.

"Now this is rain."

"This is good."

"I'm gonna go stand in the rain," I said.

"Sounds damn good," Ray said.

I turned and smiled at them. Then I went down the stairs and stood out in the parking lot in the rain. I looked up at Ray and Max, Ray smoking, Max resting his forearms on the railing, both of them smiling down at me and leaning out to get the rain on their faces.

17

Two days later I started packing up and putting my notes in order. When I went outside that afternoon, Barry, the timid man who'd tried to help me when I'd first moved in upstairs, was at the railing.

"Well, what do you think, Barry?"

"I think I'm half pissed. You want a beer?"

"Sure."

He went back in and got a can of Extra Old Stock for me and one for himself. I stood beside him at the second-floor railing drinking the beer and looking out. "Is it gonna rain again tonight?"

"Yep. Tonight it's gonna rain. The wind's changed. You get that warm air hitting the cold air. I can tell." He paused. "I'm not a weatherman, though. I don't know for sure."

"Can you always tell the weather?" I asked.

"Most of the time. Not always." He fell silent, his arms hanging at his sides. When I'd moved in upstairs and he had offered to help, he'd stood just as he was doing now, awaiting instructions.

After a minute he said: "Were you gone for a while?" He smiled shyly. "Did I ask you that before?"

"No, don't worry. Yeah, I've been gone a few days. I went to Williams Lake."

"I lived there three years," Barry said. "I didn't like it. It's a dirty town. Streets full of bars. It's an Indian town. I got nothing against Indians, mind you."

"What about Prince George?"

"Yeah, I've lived there for a bit. I don't like it. It's another dirty town."

"Kamloops?"

"I don't like it. It's another dirty town." He paused. "All that area: that's Indian country."

18

That evening on my walk the wind blew up and the sky filled with clouds. And then, just as Barry had said it would, it started to rain. Rain drops spattered on the bridge as I crossed it like sudden dark freckles. I could smell rain in the dust and warm air.

A faint blatting of jake brakes came from further up the highway.

I climbed the road. All at once it was cool. Water ran in streams along the roadcut, dragging at the dirt, making little creeks, and

I thought of my boyhood town of Hinton and my wet runners in spring that had felt so light on my feet after months of wearing winter boots.

At the top of the hill I stopped and looked down at the town. When I'd first driven into Ashcroft on the Highland Valley road, I'd stopped the car before the big descent and got out and walked to the edge of the highway and looked down. Now I sat by the side of the road and thought about the weeks that had passed. I made a circle of my thumb and forefinger and closed one eye and lifted the circle of thumb and forefinger to my other eye and stared at the town through it. Then I stood up.

By the time I reached the motel the sky had cleared. I crossed the parking lot and went up the steps and into my room. I lay on my bed and looked through the window at the clouds in the west. The sun had set, but like a fire whose original source had burnt out it flamed on the undersides of the clouds, a red so deep it reminded me of the fire that a month earlier had burnt down the no-longer-used school at the end of Railway. I remembered the flames, dark red, with no orange brightness, evil-looking, as if they had escaped from under the earth. And I remembered the spectators. In their cowboy hats and cheap shirts and jeans, they had looked from across the street like an unschooled painting representing a country scene.

19

The next morning the sky was blue. I drank coffee and packed up the last of my books and clothes. I listened to the radio. Then I went over to Wayne's to arrange a time to take pictures of him in his western gear. We decided on four, so he wouldn't feel rushed. But that afternoon when I knocked on the door he called out, "I'm just finishin' up! Hang on a sec!"

Instantly I felt irritated.

I waited. Finally Wayne shouted, "Come on in!"

I went in and he walked out of the bathroom. His eyes were anxious, but he grinned and crouched forward a bit and whipped up a hand with the forefinger out in the "gunslinger" move.

"What do you think?"

Gleaming boots. Fancy GWG "Country" jeans that showed his girth. A belt with a gold and silver buckle. A blue silk shirt and a lighter blue silk bandana worn on the side of his neck in a way that seemed dudish, almost girlish. A black hat with the brim rolled up. In these clothes he looked pathetic and impressive and strangely forlorn, like someone dressed for an occasion that had passed by. He looked like someone in a photograph snapped by a tourist.

"You look good."

We went across Railway to the siding by the tracks where a picnic table was situated among a stand of willows. Two teenagers were sitting at the table. The girl wore a white blouse and shorts, the boy wore jeans and a cowboy shirt buttoned at the cuffs. Their heads were bent over a book he was holding. And the tracks behind them, the willow branches shading them from the sun — it made up an Ashcroft version of an old illustration in a novel. As so often that summer, watching the kids I was taken into the past.

Wayne stood by a tree not too far from where the lovers sat. He frowned. His anxious eyes accentuated the pathos of his dress.

I took three pictures, two from a distance, one close up.

"Smile," I said.

"I can't. This means too much to me."

"Come on, smile."

But he couldn't.

I was abrupt, unable to keep my irritation with him out of my voice; and I hurt him. He wanted pictures of the two of us. I said, "No. You're the important one," and took my pictures and left.

Later I lay on my bed thinking about what I had done. After supper, trying to shake the mood, I walked along the path by the river I'd walked my first afternoon in Ashcroft. Now suddenly it was overgrown, grass brushing against my knees. The words "FUK OFF" had been printed in dripping white paint on one of the old fences that ran along the path.

The words seemed harsh, directed at me. I stared at them, then turned around and walked in the evening silence over the bridge, then down Railway back to my room.

Cowboy Stories

1

When I was a ten-year-old in Hinton, Alberta, part of the fascination of cowboy stories lay in the idea of the "sign." You knew that the hero was a hero not just because he looked like a hero and carried a gun; you also knew it because he could get down on one knee and read the earth. Of all his abilities, this one was the best. It gave the cowboy that aura of power that children envelop anyone with who has a technical competence beyond their own.

The drama was always pretty much the same. If he was on a horse, the cowboy would let out a low whistle, stop, and get off. Then, with the sharp attentiveness of Sherlock Holmes or Captain Cyrus Smith in *The Mysterious Island*, he would gently finger the broken branch he had spotted or else roll a cigarette as he studied the barely legible trace of a week-old hoofprint. You could almost hear the wheels going around in his head as he pondered this scrap of information.

At such moments the cowboy would be as quiet and abstracted as a mechanic. But whenever these moments appeared in cowboy stories I would tense up with delight. Because here was the clue; decipher the clue and the whole story would snap into focus.

This thrilled me. And it thrilled the first audience for Western stories as well. It provided a new image of nature, one in which an intense interest attached to its tiniest details, to "a tree stump, a beaver's den, a rock, a buffalo skin, an immobile canoe, or a floating leaf," as Balzac put it in a passage in which he expressed the enthusiasm of Parisian readers for the books of James Fenimore Cooper that were then coming out.

In fact, the details of landscape that readers found in the first Westerns fascinated them in exactly the way that clues fascinated them in the first detective stories. Here lay the interest of the "sign." It was a modern interest, and the cowboy hero was a modern type.

In the cowboy story you found an image of a man at work; and while his work was exotic, it remained work nonetheless. The cowboy could ride a horse, read signs, hunt; he could rope cattle, mend fences, and talk with Indians. His competence was total. And for me as a boy — just as for the old men who read Westerns in Ashcroft, walking slowly to the library from shacks and mobile homes that squatted like frogs on the banks of the Thompson — for them as for me, this competence was one of the most important aspects of his character.

Hence the fact that the classic cowboy story presented the hero's world as a kind of working environment, as actual as the writer could make it. Everything I'd loved as a boy in Alberta — the falling snow that turned the air grey; the strong pressure of the river against the cowboy's legs as he broke the force of the current for his pregnant wife holding onto him on the downriver side (that wife would later die); the forested hillsides that smelled of pine and cool air; the fires he made, circled with rocks on which he baked his trout — everything was presented with a deliberate matter-of-factness, as if no matter how wild and grand the landscape the cowboy only noticed it out of the corner of his eye, if he noticed it at all.

Of course, I didn't mind it when the writer allowed landscape description — a sentence or two flushed with a sunset, for instance. I wanted the cowboy's world to come alive. Above all I wanted the story to show me things that as a boy in Pocahontas and Hinton I yearned to see presented in print: what a charging bear looked like, how stormclouds developed as they came over the palisades, how you could keep warm outside while snow whirled through the night. (You slept beneath a lean-to covered with a canvas tarp that reflected the fire's radiant heat onto your back, and imagining it I could feel the warmth of that reflected heat and how the wind made the snow fly in every direction and how towards morning the snow would stop and the night sky would fill with stars.) Like the men in Ashcroft I wanted a hero who couldn't just shoot a rifle, but also rub down a horse and tell the difference between fox and rabbit scat. And in the most engrossing Westerns — the ones that most pulled me in — I got what I was looking for.

2

But what gripped me was only in part the detective-engineer side of the cowboy. Even more I was enthralled by the warrior side, the freebooting, roving mercenary side that connected the cowboy hero to a long string of heroes that went all the way back to *The Iliad*.

Like Odysseus (and all the picaresque heroes descended from him, including Conan the Barbarian and Han Solo), the cowboy was a freelance. And the shabby, down-at-heels quality of the freelance was often brought out in Westerns. But the cowboy was different, too. Already at the age of eight or nine I could see that the cynicism that tended to go along with this shabbiness wasn't really part of the Western hero. Even in a mediocre comic book like *The Two-Gun Kid* that I read with Nalbert Marchand near the muskeg past the Hinton mill, the hero evoked something sombre, something redolent of the harsh world around us, something that drew on the badly drawn yet still powerful landscapes through which he rode and that set him apart from the other comic book characters whose stories we followed.

And that summer in Ashcroft reading Cormac McCarthy's masterpiece *Blood Meridian*, I discovered the same thing: an archaic power as terrific as that in Homer's poem of war. Some writers I would later read deny this side of the Western hero. They assert, for instance, that the cowboy's attractiveness lies in his air of leisure, as if he were a Peter O'Toole in boots, a kind of aristocrat who goes around shooting people and repairing widows' fences. But I had known even as a boy that the cowboy hero "fronted" like an aboriginal convict facing a judge: his foreknowledge of death was the central fact he carried aways with him.

This was given iconic form in the hundreds of cowboy movies I saw between the ages of five and ten. At that time the old men I met who read Westerns in Ashcroft had just come back from the war; like me, they were ready to appreciate dust, an austere landscape and an archaic kind of violence. We would wait for it, and it would happen.

It was always the same. The cowboy rode slowly into town, one hand in his lap. All you could hear was the wind. On that big 1950s screen, the black and white dusty streets, the blank windows, hitching posts and bare false fronts all shouted danger, but the point of these scenes, the thing that gave them their indelible power, was that they defined the cowboy. It was just this he was meant to do — to live at just this pitch of tension and with just this much at stake. Quietly he pushed through the saloon doors and made his way through suddenly silent groups of men until he stood at the bar and in a soft voice ordered a drink. And when he finally straightened and drew he slaughtered with the same clarity of intention as Achilles on the plains of Troy.

3

In Ashcroft I often went to Frank's New and Used, an old wooden building that had once been the town's opera house. I liked to step out of the hot sunlight into the cooler darkness that smelled of dust and burlap and look at the Westerns.

Most pocket books went for a quarter. But the Westerns were seventy-five cents. Dozens of them were stacked on the old wooden planks. Their covers showed lean-jawed men in dark clothes down on one knee fanning a gun, or else riding a horse with a rifle out. I liked their titles: *Hondo, The Tall Stranger, Ride the River, Showdown at Yellow Butte.* And I liked their violence.

In Louis L'Amour's *Hondo*, for instance, I read a number of pertinent passages one hot afternoon sitting on the verandah of the Ashcroft Motel. Out in the parking lot a short, fat man in a high-crowned cowboy hat and wearing jeans that showed his socks shouted to his girlfriend: "That goddamn Joe! I told him he's gotta get out! Of course he feels lonely! Sittin' there all day watching them soaps! He's addicted to that junk!"

How genre fiction brings back the lazy days in which you read it! I marked a passage that still has the ring from my pop bottle on it:

> Turning swiftly, Hondo kicked the gun from Lowe's hand, then he grabbed him by the shirt front and jerked him to his feet. Hondo smashed a right into Lowe's stomach, then shoved him away and hit him in the face with both hands. Lowe lunged, swinging, but Hondo knocked down Lowe's right and crossed over his left. Lowe staggered and Hondo walked in. . . . Hondo slapped him. It was a power-ful, brutal slap that jarred Lowe to his heels and turned him half around.

Every word of this brings back the hot, easy days I spent that summer. The violence was risible, of course, as it always is in genre fiction; and I thought that for many readers this would make them close the book in distaste. I thought: My city friends wouldn't like this. But as the summer wore on and the pile of Westerns on my kitchen counter grew, I thought: No, it isn't the violence; what might irritate them is the hero's *innocence*, or more exactly, that combination of violence and innocence which I now realized completely shaped the cowboy hero.

The covers of my books said it all. The cowboy was bound up with his world. He couldn't be separated from it. He belonged to it as much as did the wolves and horses who shared it with him. Even his clothes showed this. Old and stale, they were faded to a neutral colour that lost itself against the dirt. When he drank from a spring he lay prone and lapped the water like an animal.

And he came awake like a cat: at the slightest movement he went
from sleep to full alertness, listening to the crunch of a twig or
the taking of a breath.

More deeply, he resembled the land. As the writers put it, his
face and body were as hard as the desert cliffs, he was as capable
of violence as a sudden flash flood, and with his combination of
tension and stillness he demanded study, and revealed sign, as
much as did the wilderness landscape itself. (In *Hondo*, a shiny
spot on Hondo's jeans told the woman observing him that Hondo
must have worn *two* guns at one time.)

Above all, the cowboy's world was hard. It could break his leg,
drown him, or make him die of thirst. As the writers said, it was
a "pitiless" world, one that maimed and killed, and that summer,
reading, I again and again found this to be so.

Consider:

> here lies a man who has just been shot off a cliff: in his fall
> he has broken so many bones he sprawls on the sharp rocks
> as askew as a cloth doll. Here sits a man on the ground
> holding a stomach wound grisly as a lithograph of war.
> And watch this rider, thrown off a horse, his foot still in
> the stirrup, being dragged along the ground until his head
> is torn half off.

And then there was *Blood Meridian*. Some passages I read two
or three times. Scene after scene presented in concentrated form
what my other books only faintly evoked:

> The . . . top of the sun rose out of nothing like the head of
> a great red phallus until it cleared the unseen rim and sat
> squat and pulsing and malevolent behind them. The shad-
> ows of the smallest stones lay like pencil lines across the
> sand and the shapes of the men and their mounts advanced
> elongate before them like strands of the night from which
> they'd ridden, like tentacles to bind them to the darkness
> yet to come. They rode with their heads down, faceless
> under their hats, like an army asleep on the march. By mid-

morning another man had died and they lifted him from the wagon where he'd stained the sacks he'd lain among and buried him also and rode on.

But though the land was hard, it contained no evil. Evil existed only in men. In none of my Westerns did I detect a trace of that theological darkness that was associated with the landscapes of crime fiction and horror. The cowboy's world was innocent. Even in *Blood Meridian*, where nature's extremes were evoked with an intensity that made the book one of the finest in American literature, it was innocent:

> The jagged mountains were pure blue in the dawn and everywhere birds twittered and the sun when it rose caught the moon in the west so that they lay opposed to each other across the earth, the sun whitehot and the moon a pale replica, as if they were the ends of a common bore beyond whose terminals burned worlds past all reckoning.

And here, I realized, when I read this evocation of nature's fundamental innocence, here I realized I had come upon the single most important thing determining the nature of the Western. I now understood why a brilliant writer like McCarthy had turned to the genre. I understood why Westerns at their best had the power of fairy tale and myth. And I knew why the cowboy story had permeated world culture. What other genre could attract the attention of both a six-year-old child and a seventy-year-old man? As I read I increasingly heard a note that brought to mind movies I had seen, like *Dersu Uzula* and *Days of Heaven*, a note that in the darkest extremity calmly stated: "This is how things are." Consider this, one of a dozen passages I marked that summer in McCarthy's book:

> On the day that followed they crossed a lake of gypsum so fine the ponies left no track upon it. The riders wore masks of bone-black smeared about their eyes and some had blacked the eyes of their horses. The sun reflected off

the pan burned the undersides of their faces and shadow of horse and rider alike were painted upon the fine white powder in purest indigo. Far out on the desert to the north dustspouts rose wobbling and augured the earth and some said they'd heard of pilgrims borne aloft like dervishes in those mindless coils to be dropped broken and bleeding upon the desert again and there perhaps to watch the thing that had destroyed them lurch onward like some drunken djinn and resolve itself once more into the elements from which it sprang. Out of that whirlwind no voice spoke and the pilgrim lying in his broken bones might cry out and in his anguish he may rage, but rage at what?

The natural world in the Western was violent and innocent, and so was the hero who inhabited it.

4

That summer I fell in love with distance. I walked up into the hills and looked out sixty kilometres across Ashcroft and the mesas beyond. I drove to Kamloops and stared out across the desert landscape, and one afternoon I drove up into the Hat Creek Valley and with the sun shining on my face saw a curtain of rain fall across the air like thin black smoke a thousand metres away.

The cowboy hero, too, swam in distance. He had his being in a world of virtually limitless space, and this had an effect on who he was and what his actions amounted to that I sensed at once but for a long time found hard to pin down in words.

It amounted to this. All his actions — from rolling a cigarette to shooting a gun — had a ceremonial significance. They occurred in a world of silence and emptiness, a world in which very little happened from one hour to the next, and so they took on that almost ritualistic quality that marks anyone's behaviour — the behaviour of an Inuit out hunting, for instance — when it appears drastically simplified in comparison to our own. Everything was stripped down and given a kind of heroic, matter-of-fact resonance.

So that whatever the cowboy hero did it seemed elemental. Whether it was making a fire or killing a man, it had no ethical or moral implications. It was as if all that distance and silence swallowed up such implications, made them beside the point, as if the Western obeyed a law that said: Where there is distance there cannot be evil.

Every Western I read that summer had this formula as its spine. In *Hondo*, Louis L'Amour had pointed to Hondo's "buried core of tenderness." But this core of tenderness — which I came to think of as the "truth" about the hero — only really showed itself in a setting of sky and distance. Seen in a crowded room, the cowboy appeared closed-in and even ordinary. But once on his horse and dwindling to a dot on the horizon, a grandeur attached to his image, as if the sky itself were memorializing him. Similarly, if the hero's sidekick died, he was buried in the open and the earth's long grass became his monument. So that emotion, poetry and innocence were all communicated in the cowboy story in terms of space and distance. Evil, however, was always a matter of rooms, the smaller the more malevolent, manmade places where intimacy took on a hellish quality and the cowboy's nature was forced to contract into something unlike itself.

But here was the problem. All this was fine in the world of the cowboy story — but only in that world. Take the cowboy hero out of his appropriate surroundings, the liberal could say, and he became an eccentric: a hardbitten egotist, with an unbounded sense of his own worth and a complete inability to communicate with anyone who didn't appreciate that worth. Certainly he was innocent; but what did this innocence amount to? Only a kind of *bon enfant* brutality that everybody else was supposed to take into account and treat with respect. He was responsible only to himself, and if he stepped in and helped somebody out, it was because he perceived that person as weaker than himself and likely to brim with gratitude at what he'd done. When there were complications, he moved on. Everything that meant collective effort was beyond him, whether it was raising a family or becoming a member of a community. True, he had a "buried core of tenderness." But the whole point about this buried core of tenderness was that it was buried. The cowboy demanded to be deciphered; he disliked talking about himself and in fact was incapable of doing so — all he could do was display himself. In intimate surroundings he fell back on a bundle of mannerisms — a way of touching his hat, a way of looking out the window — and it was the other person (the widow, the boy) who had to make the effort of communication. In the end he was vivacious only among people like himself, sidekicks who would respect his eccentricity and ask nothing of him that might impinge on his essential selfishness.

A disillusioned picture. Yet it suggested something of what happened when the image of the cowboy was held up as a model for real life. It didn't work. In contemporary urban life at any rate you couldn't be innocent and violent at the same time without appearing like a kid, with all of the kid's willful passivity, not to mention his baffled impulse towards tenderness, and a stony refusal to explain himself. If you remained adolescent into middle age you became a character, and I knew as a fact that the cowboy genre had started to break down when movies had begun to appear in which the disillusioned fighter realized that he had become a character, a kind of Peter Pan with a gun who could only be a hero to some naive teenager who wanted to be just like him.

In earlier movies the faces and bearing of the actors — say, of Randolph Scott or John Wayne — had given them an automatic authority. But by the late sixties that authority had fallen apart — the Western was seized by an irresistible impulse to parody itself. Many factors contributed to this impulse — feminism was important, and so was a widespread disgust with individuals like US general Curtis Lemay. But what they all had in common was a sense that the cowboy hero was fundamentally outdated. No one watched *Gunsmoke* anymore. Disney had stopped making movies in which dust appeared. The Western had slipped into the past.

5

Sometimes on a Saturday I'd see the older Ashcroft cowboys come down to the Safety Mart to shop. They'd limp from their trucks in the hot sun, their quilted vests accentuating their narrow old-man shoulders. Hips sore, they'd walk slowly along the sidewalk, solitary figures with gnarled hands. Native and white, leaning forward, their pale or dark eyes looked out at you from under their hatbrims. They were men who had lived their whole lives in poverty, and watching them I'd sometimes think: So these are the rednecks you hear about.

Was the cowboy story a redneck genre? Was it backward? Was its decline a "progressive" action, similar, say, to getting rid of dog fights or the hanging of criminals? Maybe so. But as the summer wore on, issues of this kind stopped interesting me. Instead I started to explore the two internal reasons that seemed to explain why Westerns were no longer read.

Genre fiction operated like fashion — it had to keep changing if it was to keep our interest. When we read genre fiction we were faithless, we followed our pleasure, just as we did when we looked at clothes. And we did so in both cases with the same eye for the often very minor novelty that excited and charmed.

But while other genres could change and stay interesting and alive because their "worlds" changed and remained alive — the "city" in detective stories, the "future" in science fiction — the world of the cowboy lay in the past, frozen. So that the genre couldn't change, couldn't develop, it seemed, except in the direction of parody.

Even more important was the fact that the Western could no longer express without parody a certain refusal of violence. As a boy I had never thought of the cowboy hero as someone who threw his weight around. In the classic Western, only the villain did that. Yet increasingly this was how male heroes acted. Whether he was Steven Segal or a rap music thug, the hero loved to say "Fuck you," loved to pull a gun from his jacket or kick out with a steel-toed boot.

And in comparison to his neon-lit menace, the Western hero could seem slow. He existed in an innocent landscape of which he was part, and at the very least this quieted his pace. You didn't just think of the cowboy hero pulling out a gun. You also thought of him mending a boot as he sat tailor-fashion before a small fire, or else lying in his blankets with his saddle under his head, staring at the stars. Connected to childhood and the natural world in a way that the modern hero wasn't, the cowboy's reflectiveness was part of his dignity, and it drew its authority from the landscape through which he moved.

But now that landscape had altered — or more exactly, our perception of it had altered. And that summer I came to realize just how much this was so.

6

During my time in Ashcroft I was often happy. In a way that seemed uncanny, my childhood returned to me. Some mornings, waking to desert sun and a quiet outside that the voices of the old men on the verandah only deepened, a joy touched me that I hadn't known in years.

But other times I felt more complicated emotions. One evening in late July, around nine o'clock, the hot sun down and a softening darkness on the hills, I went into Tom's Videos along with Henry Maurice, a well-known roper and friend of Ray's who had retired and now lived in an apartment up on the mesa.

Maybe because I was with him, and he felt it I would expect it of him, or maybe because he actually wanted to do it, Henry walked over to the Westerns. He looked through them. After a bit, he said, "I don't know why, but they don't make 'em anymore like they used to."

"Aw, Henry, don't give up," I said.

"I'm not givin' up. That's not my point."

"Okay, sorry. So what d'you wanna get?"

He shrugged and picked slowly through the boxes, not looking at me.

I picked out *High Plains Drifter* and immediately felt like I was being pushy.

"I've seen it." Henry picked up the box and looked at it. He seemed embarrassed. "I guess I could see it again."

Outside night was in the air and the street was silent. As we walked back to the motel I thought about Henry's embarrassment.

It may have had to do with me and how I had acted. But there was something else there too. Come across an old Western in a video store and it did seem embarrassing, even sad. And I realized, as we walked beside the Canadian Pacific tracks that night, that what had most doomed the genre wasn't its structural limitations or its lack of casual violence. (Describing the current movie scene, Geoffrey O'Brien summed it up as "Pepsi, an exploding head, and you.") What had most doomed it was the belated, post-World-War-Two euphoria that first swept across TV screens in the sixties. Combined with widescreen movies and the hedonistic intoxication of the period, this euphoria — and the *Seinfeld* irony it later turned into — had produced a new feeling in popular culture, one that made the fatalistic legends of the West seem outdated. Pushed aside by *I Spy*, the cowboy landscape had become a dustbowl that only the irrigation of colour and fun could restore to life. Nowadays a straight Western seemed claustrophobic; and so Henry, sitting in his apartment, could find images of the life he had lived only in barbecue sauce ads or reruns of *City Slickers*. "Nature, today, is the city," Roland Barthes once wrote; and it seemed to me that night that the decline of the cowboy story showed this as well as any other phenomenon.